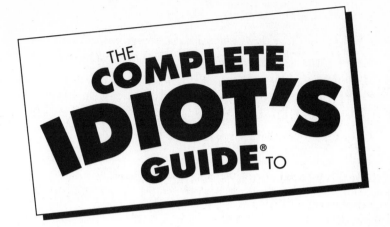

THE COMPLETE IDIOT'S GUIDE® TO

Connecting with Your Angels

by Cecily Channer with Damon Brown

D1444072

ALPHA

A member of Penguin Group (USA) Inc.

Cecily: For Todd and our new angel baby
Damon: For my spiritual mentors, both past and present

ALPHA BOOKS

Published by the Penguin Group

Penguin Group (USA) Inc., 375 Hudson Street, New York, New York 10014, USA

Penguin Group (Canada), 90 Eglinton Avenue East, Suite 700, Toronto, Ontario M4P 2Y3, Canada (a division of Pearson Penguin Canada Inc.)

Penguin Books Ltd., 80 Strand, London WC2R 0RL, England

Penguin Ireland, 25 St. Stephen's Green, Dublin 2, Ireland (a division of Penguin Books Ltd.)

Penguin Group (Australia), 250 Camberwell Road, Camberwell, Victoria 3124, Australia (a division of Pearson Australia Group Pty. Ltd.)

Penguin Books India Pvt. Ltd., 11 Community Centre, Panchsheel Park, New Delhi—110 017, India

Penguin Group (NZ), 67 Apollo Drive, Rosedale, North Shore, Auckland 1311, New Zealand (a division of Pearson New Zealand Ltd.)

Penguin Books (South Africa) (Pty.) Ltd., 24 Sturdee Avenue, Rosebank, Johannesburg 2196, South Africa

Penguin Books Ltd., Registered Offices: 80 Strand, London WC2R 0RL, England

Copyright © 2009 by Cecily Channer and Damon Brown

International Standard Book Number: 978-1-59257-878-8
Library of Congress Catalog Card Number: 2009920700

11 10 09   8 7 6 5 4 3 2 1

Interpretation of the printing code: The rightmost number of the first series of numbers is the year of the book's printing; the rightmost number of the second series of numbers is the number of the book's printing. For example, a printing code of 09-1 shows that the first printing occurred in 2009.

Printed in the United States of America

Note: This publication contains the opinions and ideas of its authors. It is intended to provide helpful and informative material on the subject matter covered. It is sold with the understanding that the authors and publisher are not engaged in rendering professional services in the book. If the reader requires personal assistance or advice, a competent professional should be consulted.

The authors and publisher specifically disclaim any responsibility for any liability, loss, or risk, personal or otherwise, which is incurred as a consequence, directly or indirectly, of the use and application of any of the contents of this book.

Most Alpha books are available at special quantity discounts for bulk purchases for sales promotions, premiums, fundraising, or educational use. Special books, or book excerpts, can also be created to fit specific needs.

For details, write: Special Markets, Alpha Books, 375 Hudson Street, New York, NY 10014.

Publisher: *Marie Butler-Knight*
Editorial Director: *Mike Sanders*
Senior Managing Editor: *Billy Fields*
Executive Editor: *Randy Ladenheim-Gil*
Development Editor: *Lynn Northrup*
Production Editor: *Kayla Dugger*

Copy Editor: *Tricia S. Liebig*
Cover Designer: *Bill Thomas*
Book Designer: *Trina Wurst*
Indexer: *Tonya Heard*
Layout: *Ayanna Lacey*
Proofreader: *Laura Caddell*

Contents at a Glance

Contents

Foreword

I met Cecily Channer in the early stages of her search for spiritual truth and enlightenment. Her unusual experiences inspired her to explore the unseen world of angels. Cecily's passion for knowledge led her to study with experts in the field of angelic communication and spirituality. Since her first sighting of angelic energy, she has emerged as a leader in the world of angelic communication. Now she shares her insights to benefit others, change perceptions, and give hope that we are never alone, as angels are always with us.

Many turn to their celestial helpers in a time of need, sorrow, or fear. While it is true they will listen and act upon your requests (if possible), they remain steady and strong throughout all of your life experiences. Their daily interactions are personal and clearly visible once you have established a connection with them. Have you ever wondered to whom you are speaking when you rant and rave to an otherwise empty room?

In the decades I have been working with the angelic force, I have come to learn they are major contributors to our lives. Just imagine a host of angels listening to you, understanding you, and comforting you through difficult times—sometimes doing nothing more than holding your spirit steady as you right yourself. They do not need to be your silent partners on your path, but rather interactive and dependable allies.

We must always remember the key to unlocking the door of angelic communication is intent and belief. The intent must be pure and led by the idea of helping others (or even the seeker), to heal their spirits and be better human beings. Belief not just in angels themselves, but also that we have the right and the instinctual ability to connect with them. They were given to us as guiding forces, confidants, and friends. Who could ask for more?

As a teacher I learned a long time ago that every student learns differently, and the same is true of angelic communication. Everyone finds the connection method that works best for him or her. For some it is as simple as just believing in their existence and thus an automatic and natural connection takes place. For others it may be more complicated, but accessible nonetheless. The spiritual peace and sense of fellowship is worth any effort required.

Discovering how you as an individual will interact with your angels is the key to successful communications. Personally I "hear" the angels. Do I hear them in a distinct and booming voice? No. Their voice is my voice. In my head I will hear things in my own voice. It is the texture, the timbre that varies. This is a core basis for my own teaching. Angels don't have vocal cords; therefore, they will use whatever method you are open to "hearing" to communicate with you. Is it color, or certain animals that come into your life, or perhaps a song with a message that plays everywhere you go? Regardless of how you "hear," they will find a way to get their messages of hope, inspiration, and love to you. Quickly discovering your modality for communication is key.

The Complete Idiot's Guide to Connecting with Your Angels offers the reader a full course of angelic information and techniques to aid in manifesting that connection. Regardless of your level of angelic knowledge, this book has something to offer the beginner, intermediate, or even advanced student of enlightenment.

For the beginner, basic angelic principles and history are presented in a clear and concise manner to allow the novice to discover the world of angels. Many "how to" techniques are explained and demonstrated.

Intermediate students are assured growth opportunities as well. This work introduces new and innovative methods for angelic connection. Regardless of the level of previous learning or the method used by the intermediate, this work will encourage the reader to explore new depths with their communication abilities.

Advanced students of angelic communication are also given the gift of fresh ideas and meditations. The authors strive to provide various pathways by sharing their personal guided meditations with us. I learned more than a few new methods while reading this work.

Tina Michelle
Angel Interpreter, Medium, and Spiritual Teacher

Introduction

As a spiritual teacher and intuitive, Cecily does not live your average life—nor would she want to. For the last seven years, the angels have been her daily companions giving her lots of guidance, love, and comfort, and as a result, Cecily's world has gone from black and white to technicolor (sometimes literally!). Cecily sees the angels as a loving presence in her life, watching over her and offering kindness and inspiration. Since she invited the angels into her life, she has experienced more joy, beauty, and peace. Cecily's experiences with the angelic realm may sound extraordinary to some, but in all honesty the magic of the spiritual realms is open to everyone. Experiences may vary from person to person, but rest assured—when you open the door to the divine, anything can happen!

Cecily was not born a mystic or seer; she was essentially a normal girl who grew up to have some very out-of-this-world experiences. In fact, she never thought too much about the angels until her quest for spiritual truth brought them auspiciously into her life one day. Yet it was her early childlike wonder that stayed with her over the years and opened her mind and heart to see beyond our limited three-dimensional reality. Cecily's childhood love of the magical and whimsical gave her a deep longing to connect with the unseen world that surrounds us.

The "spiritual" Beatle, George Harrison, said it so well in one of his last interviews. Here is the gist of what he said: "If you are not questioning why you're here on Earth, what is the point of being here at all?"

This was Cecily's mantra as an adult and led her to her first spiritual teacher back in 2001. At that time, Cecily was looking for more guidance on how she could create a better life for herself and decided to consult someone who might have some answers for her. Guidance came in the form of a gifted spiritual teacher named Tina Michelle. Tina was in town for the weekend doing readings at a local spiritually based bookstore and when Cecily saw an advertisement for her she experienced a deep knowing that she needed to see her. Cecily knew nothing about her, other than she had been a featured guest on several television shows. As it turned out, she didn't even know that Tina Michelle worked with the angelic realm until she met with her. When Cecily first sat down with Tina for her reading, she was struck by Tina's easy manner, charming Southern accent, and humor, and was immediately put at ease. As the reading progressed, Cecily was blown away, not only by Tina's ability to describe what was already happening in her life, but by her amazing way of bringing forth much-needed insight and guidance about how she could make her life more fulfilling. Where was she getting such clear and loving information? Cecily had to know. Tina told her that it came from her ability to communicate directly with the angels of the person she was reading for. She had been communicating directly with Cecily's guardian angels. What a concept! Immediately intrigued, Cecily decided that she wanted to learn how to do the same thing. At that time, Cecily didn't know what a huge catalyst this meeting would be for her.

At Tina Michelle's invitation, Cecily became her student. Now under the tutelage of her very first spiritual teacher, she could learn the ins and outs of connecting with the angels. Within months of opening up her lines of communication with the angelic realm, Cecily was given the opportunity to train under the renowned angel expert and author, Doreen Virtue. After a one-day workshop that Cecily attended, Doreen told the attendees that she had been divinely guided to offer her first and only angel therapy certification training outside of California. It would be in Chicago in the coming months (Cecily's hometown). Cecily didn't even have to think about it. She would be there! The angels seemed to be showing her the way to a better life with each passing day.

Cecily certainly wasn't prepared for the way in which her connection with the angelic realm would grow stronger and evolve since that first meeting with Tina Michelle. On December 2, 2001, Cecily had a profound spiritual experience that changed her life for good. She was visited by an angel. Following is the experience recorded in her journal the very next day.

December 2, 2001

Around 3 A.M. I was awakened from a deep sleep. I opened my eyes to see an amazing vision. On the right side of my body was a large angel! The angel appeared as a large orb of light which included all the colors of the spectrum. On either side of this orb, were large, flapping, white feathered wings. The angel flew above me and hovered for only a couple of seconds, before it disappeared and a clairvoyant picture show ran in my mind's eye. As if the movie was composed of black-and-white sketches, I saw a smiling angel flying above trees and nature. The angel appeared in a female form, but was a very crude sketch and the face appeared as a "happy face"- :). I have read that angels can take any form and they often appear in the least intimidating way possible, so that they do not frighten the seer. The "picture show" was suddenly over and I looked up to magically see hundreds of these "happy face" angels staring down at me. This was a miracle to me. I had been visited by angels, and my life would never be the same. Angels are real. There is no doubt in my mind that God exists.

After this deeply transforming encounter with the angels, Cecily knew there was more to life than the limited experience of our five senses, and couldn't look back as she was swept up in the beauty of a new more expanded realm of possibilities. Tina Michelle had assured her that everyone could communicate with the angelic realm if they opened their heart to the angels around them; it was not just for a select few. Everyone could be a mystic in their own unique way, because everyone has their own intuitive gifts. It was this knowledge that prompted her to learn to teach, heal, and inspire those seeking spiritual guidance and a daily connection with their angels. As Cecily had hoped to, she went on to complete the Angel Therapy practitioner training with Doreen Virtue, and then continued her intuitive training with the wonderfully gifted spiritual teacher and author, Sonia Choquette. All these years later, Cecily is a spiritual teacher herself, enjoying the process of assisting others in awakening to their highest potential and sharing her wisdom in *The Complete Idiot's Guide to Connecting with Your Angels*.

Even though Cecily will always be on a serious quest for spiritual knowledge, the angels have helped her lighten up in her daily life. One of Cecily's favorite quotes is "Angels can fly, because they take themselves lightly."

How to Use This Book

This book is divided into three main parts:

Part 1, "Meet the Angels," is a warm welcome to this supportive group that helps us along our life's journey. Consider it the ultimate primer to what the angels are and what they do.

Part 2, "Angel Messages," will get you communicating with the angels. We'll show you how to open up more doors to the angelic realm and how to hear their guidance.

Part 3, "Working with the Angels," takes your angelic knowledge to the next level. The more in-depth techniques here include spiritual rituals and information on the special bonds between the angels and children. Plus, you'll learn how the angels can assist us in our love lives.

We also have five helpful appendixes for your reference. Appendix A breaks down the many spiritual terms you need to know. Appendix B answers your angel FAQs quickly. Oracle cards, which can help you connect with your angels, are discussed in Appendix C. It's sometimes important to be fully proactive and engaged to communicate, as we explain in Appendix D on angel field trips. Finally, the online and literary resources in Appendix E encourage you to continue your journey for knowledge beyond this book.

Extras

When it comes to the angels, the more you know, the higher you can fly with them! We've added some fun tidbits and info within each chapter under the following headings:

Angels 101

Here you'll find tips, hints, and insights to help make communicating with the angels easier.

def•i•ni•tion

Check these boxes for definitions of spiritual or angelic words that may be unfamiliar to you.

Enlightenments

Check these boxes for fun, interesting history, related information, and trivia that will make your angelic knowledge that much more impressive.

Advice from Above

These are warnings about confusing or hard-to-understand details about the angels, as well as helpful hints about how to avoid angelic missteps and misunderstandings.

Acknowledgments

Cecily would like to thank her husband, Todd Schmid, and her good friends Jennifer Calligan, Suzanne Morrison, Polly Lamers, Nicole Gifford, Felicia Libbin, and Kris Tait for all their support. She would also like to dedicate this book to her beloved spiritual teachers Sonia Choquette and Tina Michelle.

Damon would like to thank his mom, Bernadette Johnson, and his father and stepfather, David G. Brown and Tony Howard, as well as his girlfriend, Dr. Parul Patel. Most importantly, he dedicates this book to his spiritual mentors, including Rosemary "Roro" Taylor, and spiritual authors before him, particularly Linda Goodman.

Trademarks

All terms mentioned in this book that are known to be or are suspected of being trademarks or service marks have been appropriately capitalized. Alpha Books and Penguin Group (USA) Inc. cannot attest to the accuracy of this information. Use of a term in this book should not be regarded as affecting the validity of any trademark or service mark.

Part 1

Meet the Angels

In Part 1, we learn about the angels: what they are, what their purpose is, and how they can assist us on our life journey. Knowing their history will help you communicate with them better. We also break down the incorrect (and sometimes humorous) myths about the angels, go over the different types of angels, and discuss the Spiritual Support Team—a wonderful group that is often confused with the angels themselves. Part 1 is the perfect primer for angel newbies and heavenly experts alike.

Help from a Higher Power

In This Chapter

- Defining what an angel is
- Learning an angel's main objectives
- Discovering the three major types of angels
- Understanding the angels and free will

We are living in a sophisticated time, surrounded by iPhones and TiVos, telecommunications and online blogs. So many new technologies have taken over our modern civilization.

Regardless of our worldly needs and high-speed lives, we want to connect to a higher power. A recent Gallup Poll found that 82 percent of women and 72 percent of men believe in angels today. Despite war, poverty, and ongoing inhumanity, we still believe that we are being watched, we are being protected, and perhaps we are being loved by higher beings.

What Is an Angel?

An angel is an eternal spiritual being sent from a higher power—often referred to as God, Allah, or the Source—with orders to guide us into peace and love. They have been around for millennia, well before humans were around.

Important Missions Both Great and Small

Today, the day-to-day missions of the *angels* may be as large as helping two warring political leaders see eye to eye, or as small as healing a rocky relationship between a daughter and a father. The angels actually don't have *free will*, so all their goals and actions are mandated by God.

def•i•ni•tion

> An **angel** is an eternal spiritual guide and messenger, under a higher power, sent to help humanity. **Free will** is the philosophical idea that you have the freedom to do what you want when you want without being constrained by a determined fate.

No Humans Here

Unlike popular artistic depictions, the angels do not necessarily have gigantic wings, youthful or cherubic features, or even human bodies at all. The angels are not human and have never been human. They are androgynous, egoless creatures. (Essentially, they are the very opposite of humans!) Their main goal is to help, protect, and heal, and to raise the consciousness level of all humanity.

Of the Spirit Realm

They are of spirit, not flesh, so there are no limitations to what they can do or where they can go, as long as their actions are decreed from a higher power. The angels do not work within the boundaries of time and space because they are made of pure energy. Some angels come and go, but they can be ever present in every moment of your life.

Nondenominational Beings

Aside from their love for humanity, the most wonderful thing about the angels is that they do not belong to a particular religious sect. Despite their prominence in biblical interpretations, the angels are not strictly Christian, nor, as mentioned earlier, of a particular gender or race. They are nondenominational, spiritual beings, and in that sense, people of all religious and spiritual paths can find a way to connect and communicate with their own personal angels. In short, the angels are Universal.

What Do the Angels Do?

Sure, the angels are great to have around, but what exactly do they do? The angels have three primary objectives in your life:

- ◆ Help
- ◆ Protect
- ◆ Heal

There are bigger, broader goals for humanity at large, but these are how the angels influence you the most.

Help

The first goal of an angel is to help humanity, or more specifically, to help you. Does something ever go so smoothly that it feels like it was destined to happen? Some things in life seem effortless.

Because we have free will, the angels cannot help us with a specific matter until we decide to request help from them. Unless we are to die before our time, it's against an angel's nature to do anything that would contradict our gift of free will. This, of course, requires letting the

Angels 101

Do you ever try to quiet your mind and, suddenly, you know exactly what to do? It could be your guardian angel whispering in your ear.

angels become a part of your life. Praying to God is one way to call upon the angels. The angels are willing to work up a proverbial sweat to help you, as their main goal is to get you where you need to be spiritually and emotionally. And, in turn, you help humanity by getting to where you need to be. We discuss this more in Chapter 7.

Angels 101

Do you ever feel as though roadblocks keep preventing you from doing something you desire? This is probably an angel's doing as well! Sometimes what we believe is a good move will lead to our detriment, and vice versa. The angels are tapped into the ultimate knowledge, so they know where we're going and what will happen if we continue on our current path. Life isn't meant to be easy, but the next time circumstances seem ridiculously hard, remember that your angels may be trying to open your eyes to a better path.

Protect

Another primary goal is to protect humanity, which, more often than not, means protecting humanity from itself. It is no small irony that wars are often fought over religion, the supposed home of the angels sent to protect us. In reality, the angels never condone war, and their agenda is to usher humanity into an era of peace.

On a personal level, the angels are here to constantly remind us that we are derived from greatness and that we should love others, and ourselves, regardless of our differences. When called upon, they protect us from judgment and prejudice.

Heal

An angel's final primary goal is to heal humanity. Healing humanity begins with you. As politicians often say, the only way to win an election is to get one voter at a time. If the legion of angels is following a higher power's orders to bring about world peace, it must first help the individual find that peace within himself or herself.

The more often you invite the angels into your life, the more they can help heal the relationship between you and yourself, your fellow man, and your environment.

Advice from Above

There is a popular misconception that the angels were more visible or more present during biblical times because they were more necessary at the time. Not true! Our awareness of the angels may have dropped in modern times, but the presence of the angels has not. If the main goal of the angels is to create world peace, then obviously there is more work to be done. Passionate and tireless, the angels will not stop their efforts until the job is done.

Types of Angels

There are three major types of angels:

- Guardian angels

- Archangels

- Helper angels

Angels come in various forms with specific duties. The ever-present guardian angels, the all-encompassing Archangels, and the helper angels all make sure you receive the help, protection, and healing you need.

There is also a group of spiritual beings separate from the angels, which we call the Spiritual Support Team, that also help get things done. You'll read all about them in Chapter 4.

Guardian Angels

Assigned to us before we are born, guardian angels are around every day to help us in our transition from birth to death. This isn't to say they are helping us die—heavens no!—but that they are helping us live our lives to the fullest.

However, the amount of influence they have in our lives is a choice we make. As you'll discover, other angels can be more direct, if not assertive, in helping you on your way. Guardian angels are ever present, but as with all other angels, they respect the most human of gifts: free will.

You usually have a few guardian angels—two or three—and sometimes their subtle messages are what the average person might chalk up to a simple hunch or gut feeling. (Though, of course, some feelings are just that: feelings.) Do you ever get the strange feeling that you shouldn't go to that party tonight? Or, perhaps, that eerie sense of dread that something has happened to a loved one, and the feeling that you should check on them right away? It may be the nudge of a guardian angel. And, similar to other communications, it tends to get muddied if we are blocking our emotional expression. In higher terms, guardian angels have a harder time cutting through our energy field when our emotions are high and turbulent, which is why it is crucial to center yourself to keep the communication lines open. We will discuss this in Chapter 6.

Other angels may come and go, but our guardian angels are our constant companions. Their most important role is protecting and guiding us on our journey through life. We actually meet our guardian angels before we begin our earthly lives, but for the sake of free will, our memory of them is erased. However, they remember who *we* are: our areas of growth, our strengths, and our life mission. One of the things that makes the angels beautiful is a lack of judgment, and guardian angels are ever present no matter how dark the road nor how you decide to live your life. Of course, it is our choice whether we would like to use their wisdom to make our lives better.

Enlightenments

Some believe that, before we are born, we choose the people we want to have in our lives, including our family members and closest friends. Choosing or accepting the best angels in our lives is part of this process.

Archangels

Perhaps the most dramatized of the angels, Archangels are the bigwigs. Created at the beginning of time, their main goal is to usher in peace on Earth. This is done one person at a time.

Archangels organize the other angels, directing them where needed. At the same time, they aren't afraid to get their hands dirty, so to speak. In fact, Archangels are known for getting involved, coming in immediately and acting swiftly when called upon.

When we invite the Archangels into our life, they are often behind those paradigm shifts—major insights or changes—that occur without warning. For instance, imagine running late for work because the breakfast got burnt, your favorite shirt is dirty, and you suddenly can't find your keys, just to narrowly miss the train—and it isn't until later that you find out that the train had an accident. You may come to find that near misses, close calls, or so-called lucky breaks may just be the Archangels looking out for you. They like doing big things that help you understand the precious gift of life and, sometimes, to remind you that you are being protected and loved from above.

Spiritual teacher Doreen Virtue calls the Archangels "managers" that help supervise and organize the other angels on Earth. Strong in personality, there are four well-known Archangels: Archangel Michael, Archangel Gabriel, Archangel Raphael, and Archangel Uriel. There are also three lesser-known Archangels: Archangel Chamuel, Archangel Jophiel, and Archangel Zadkiel.

Archangel Michael is the most frequently drawn Archangel. He's usually shown as a tall, young angel with gigantic wings coming down to Earth with sword in hand. Swords are usually symbolic of knowledge, not violence.

We will dive deeper into the complex personalities and strengths of the Archangels in Chapter 3.

Helper Angels

The helper angels are on the front line on the spiritual front—the worker bees of the angelic hive—and are part of the angelic team. Helper angels have very simple missions. If you have a particular issue at hand, you can ask "What angels want to work with me on this issue?" And they are at your disposal!

Advice from Above

The angels want to support you, but you're still going to be doing the work! Don't expect to be lazy and assume the angels will help you breeze through your problems. Their goal is to promote spiritual growth, not solve your problems for you.

Here are some examples:

- ◆ The Angel of Patience when you are anxious
- ◆ The Angel of Peace when you are in a conflict
- ◆ The Angel of Courage when you must take a risk

… and so on. They are your personal on-call staff to aid you in times of need.

And don't worry about burdening them—there are an infinite number of angels to call upon for any concern you may have in your life.

The Least You Need to Know

- ◆ The angels are not aligned with a particular religion. Angels are Universal.
- ◆ The angels are androgynous, egoless beings that have never been human.
- ◆ There are three primary types of angels: guardian angels, Archangels, and helper angels.
- ◆ Out of respect for your free will, the angels rarely interfere in your life if you object.

Chapter 2

Angel Myths and Truths

In This Chapter

- ◆ Addressing the myths about how the angels look
- ◆ Seeing the angels doesn't mean you're hallucinating!
- ◆ Discovering how the angels interact with humans
- ◆ Finding that there's nothing "new age" about the angels

When it comes to the amount of myths in our culture, the angels are right up there with Bigfoot and the Loch Ness Monster. Do they have wings 12 feet wide? Can they walk through walls, but only if you let them in? Talk about confusing!

The angels are real, and therefore there are very real truths ... and very real myths.

In this chapter, we discuss several age-old myths about the angels, including halos and wings, their part in hallucinations, and whether they fit into the category of "new age."

Seeing the Angels

When you think about it, the angels are as much a part of our modern pop culture as they were in biblical times. Unfortunately, there are more misconceptions today than ever. Here is a breakdown of what is true and what is misunderstood about the angels.

Myth: All Angels Are Young Men or Women

Based on common beliefs, the angels resemble young, virile men or gorgeous, delicate women à la Brad Pitt and Angelina Jolie. These ideas come from classic art, when Italian artists dramatized angelic interactions with beautiful cherubs or gorgeous young adults.

This is not true at all—the angels have gotten the Hollywood treatment!

As we mentioned in Chapter 1, the angels appear in the form you are most comfortable with, whether it be a wise old man or a funny, cute little girl. They, however, are not human. The angels are androgynous—that is, sexless—spiritual beings, and they predate humans. Some are several millennia old.

def•i•ni•tion

Anthropomorphism is the practice of giving human characteristics to a nonhuman being or object.

They are otherworldly beings made up of pure positive energy, but, perhaps so we can relate to what they are, people have historically *anthropomorphized* angels, making them seem less similar to heavenly beings and more similar to humans with superpowers.

Myth: All Angels Have a Halo and Wings

A common myth is that all angels have a bright yellow halo and fluffy, pearly white wings wide enough to wrap around you.

The angels do not have wings. Unlike humans, the angels are not limited by time and space—they can appear in multiple places at once—so the wings concept may have started as a crude way to explain how quickly they can move from place to place.

As for the halo, there is actually some truth to that: being pure energy, the angels naturally have a glow. As with a rainbow, the angels emit every color known to man, sparkling and brightening environments with their energy. They glow, but it isn't restricted to a symbolic circle floating over their heads.

That said, the angels sometimes do show themselves to us in the "classic" form with halo and wings, but this is only to make us feel comfortable. Wings are used as a symbol of comfort, and intuitively we can sometimes feel angel feathers touching us or wings embracing us.

Angels 101

Being heavenly spirits, the angels work in a higher vibration than humans—hence the wonderful, bountiful glow and the ability to move beyond our earthly limits of time and space. The more centered your energy, the more receptive you can be to an angel's efforts to communicate.

Myth: Seeing the Angels Means You're Having Hallucinations

Paranoid schizophrenia and other similar mental illnesses have traits that include delusions and hallucinations. It is as if the walls between the imagination, memory, and perception all melt away and create a current reality that never has been and probably never will be. That said, all visions or occurrences outside our normal experience do not necessarily indicate mental illness is at play. Since ancient times, seemingly lucid and fully functioning people have had visits from and sightings of the angels.

For instance, there is a clear difference between an angel sighting and a hallucination. In fact, studies have found instances of a stranger helping someone in danger and, just as suddenly, disappearing from sight. Normal, well-adjusted people have no reason to make something up, particularly if their lives were saved!

It is equally inaccurate to lump the angels into the same category as children's stories or folklore. The Bible and other documentation follow these helpful spiritual guides through history. And, depending on a personal belief system, one wouldn't be hard-pressed to find occasions where "happy coincidences" lead to a positive, life-changing event. *Serendipity* can be blamed only so many times, and the positive influence the angels have in our lives is certainly not a hallucination.

def•i•ni•tion

Serendipity is finding that things are working extremely highly in your favor without your intervention—that is, out of "coincidence."

The Relationship with Humans

Based on our pop culture, the angels are people we know who have passed on: the spirit of our Aunt Clarise swoops down to protect us from harm, or the apparition of our Granddad Burt appears to lead us in the right direction. The popular Demi Moore movie *Ghost* (1990) is totally based on this premise, as her deceased husband, played by Patrick Swayze, comes back to rescue her from his murderer. Modern interpretations are entertaining but not *totally* accurate! Deceased loved ones can help, but they do not have as much power or knowledge as the angels.

Myth: The Angels Are Former Humans

By definition, the angels are not human and have never been human. They are watchful, helpful spirits created by God. An angel may take human form—if it would help communicate with you better—but they are and always will be a healing light from God.

Enlightenments

Although the angels have never been human, there are spiritual guides who used to be human, as well as deceased loved ones who look out for you. They are part of your Spiritual Support Team, which we discuss in Chapter 4.

Myth: The Angels Come Down from Heaven Only When Necessary

It can be easy to picture a gaggle of winged angels sitting on high on their fluffy white clouds, looking down at us humans bumbling our way through the day. And perhaps, if one of us begs enough or is in an obviously horrendous enough situation, they'll discuss amongst themselves if they should come down, and maybe which should come, and, most importantly, how much they should interfere in the first place. This scenario would follow the vein of classic material similar to Greek mythology—Zeus and Hera arguing over the puny humans below—and other god-based philosophies.

The angels, however, are quite the opposite. They move among us. They are of the people. They want to get involved. The legions of angels were not created to sit around as people suffer, but to get involved. If anything, they would like to play a *bigger* part in our lives.

Myth: The Angels Will Come Only When You're Desperate

The angels seem infinitely busy. There is always a war going on somewhere, and in that war there are many people fighting for their lives or fighting to take the lives of others. Those people obviously need some help to find inner peace and, ideally, a resolution. There are people with deteriorating health, suddenly crippled from an accident, suffering from a long-term illness, or born with birth defects; obviously, they need guidance, protection, and help on their journey. Then there are the very poor, the neglected, and the millions if not billions of people of this world suffering this very second.

In light of the world's daily suffering, is it surprising that we feel guilty, ashamed, or unworthy of calling upon our angels?

The truth is the angels always have time for us. In fact, the angels are often frustrated because they would love to come in and help, but because they only follow the will of God and the individual, they must be invited into our lives to actually make a significant impact.

Also, the angels are not stifled by our limitations, so they can help multiple people at once. Made of energy, an angel can assist in one place, observe in another, and do something else in an entirely different location.

Myth: The Angels Will Stop You from Doing Bad Things

There is a wonderful, albeit inaccurate, cultural image of an angel on one shoulder and a devil on the other battling it out for a human's soul. It's a great representation of the human conscience, the conflict between doing what is easy and doing what is right. However, it is an *inner* conflict, not an outer one.

In reality, the angels cannot force you to do something you absolutely don't want to do. They carry out God's wishes, and one of God's wishes is that humans have the opportunity to decide the life they would like to lead—in short, this is free will, God's gift to man. Stepping in before you, for instance, mistreat another person, would be a violation of your free will because you decided to mistreat this person based on your own judgment. The angel does not judge, but only acts based on God's wishes and your requests.

Advice from Above

Remember, the angels can help multiple people at once. Don't be afraid to call on an angel; assisting you won't take the angel away from helping someone else also in need.

The angels will not argue with you, but they will try to lead you in the best direction for your individual spiritual growth. If you feel like you are being led in a certain direction, by all means listen!

History

The angels are not of new times, nor are they strictly relevant in the past. Here we dispel some myths about angelic history.

Myth: The Angels Are a "New Age" Phenomenon

As with any age with uncertain wars and economic woes, the new millennium has brought about more and more people looking for spiritual guidance and wisdom. People often rely on faith when things don't seem under their control.

Some may call a higher acknowledgment of the angels "new age," lumping our heavenly helpers in with all the preconceived notions that go along with that term. In some circles, new age spirituality has been deemed any spiritual practice or belief thought to be "way out there." Of course, this is a narrow view of new age spirituality and a very narrow view of the angels.

Although there is no harm in the other beliefs, there is nothing new about the presence of the angels. The angels were discussed before our lifetimes—in fact, well before the Bible itself—and the angels have been around since the beginning of time. Furthermore, the angels have been *recognized* by humans before our generation.

Advice from Above

The modern "new age" category has grown to include anything not exclusively Christian that requires a modicum of faith, including astrology, Tarot, numerology, past lives, collective consciousnesses, mind over matter, acupuncture, alternative healing, and, yes, angels. It is unfair and inaccurate to lump these diverse beliefs and practices together, as they all have very separate histories, rituals, and value systems—not to mention that none of them are new!

Myth: The Angels Were Visible Only in Biblical Times

Although the angels can often mistakenly be labeled "new age," they ironically can also be dismissed as relics of the past. There are countless references to the angels in the 2,000 years since Christ's birth.

Furthermore, if they did not have a part of our common life and consciousness, the angels would have fallen away from our culture as much as water walkers, lepers, and the alchemy of turning water into wine.

Instead, the angels are firmly planted in our commercials, our books, and our art. In short, they have not gone anywhere.

The Least You Need to Know

◆ The angels do not wear a halo, but they do emit a warm, loving glow wherever they go.

◆ The angels were never human. They were created at the beginning of time.

◆ The angels are not hallucinations, as they play a major part in those serendipitous "happy coincidences" throughout our lives.

◆ The angels are never too busy to help and enjoy participating in our spiritual growth in matters, no matter how small.

◆ The angels have not dwindled since the biblical age, as evidenced in how often we discuss them in modern culture.

Chapter 3

The Angels, the Archangels, and the Bible

In This Chapter

- ◆ Remembering notable angel appearances in the Bible
- ◆ Learning the angels' role in the birth of Jesus
- ◆ Reviewing the Archangels' different jobs and motivations
- ◆ Meeting the Archangels, cherubim, and seraphim

Whether it is helping us through a rough day or guiding us in our life's goals, the angels have different roles in our lives. A great place to start understanding them is the Bible, which gives us perspective by discussing their actions in the past, the purpose of the Archangels, and the variety of angels supporting us on our journey.

Angels in the Bible

The angels play a part in Judaism, Islam, and other major religions. However, many Americans tie the angels closest to the Bible.

There are a plethora of angel appearances in the Bible—indeed, it could be a book in itself!—so in this chapter, we highlight the most notable angel stories in the classic text.

First Mention of the Angels in the Bible (Genesis 3:24)

Then God said, "Now that the man has become like one of us in knowing good from evil, he must not be allowed to reach out his hand and pick from the tree of life, too, and eat and live for ever!" / So God expelled him from the Garden of Eden, to till the soil from which he had been taken / He banished the man, and in front of the Garden of Eden he posted the great winged creatures and the fiery flashing sword, to guard the way to the tree of life. (Genesis 3:22–24)

> **Enlightenments**
>
> Although some have argued that Adam, not Eve, actually picked the fruit from the tree of life, scholars now aren't sure what fruit it was. The King James Bible—the most cited version of the book—never specifically says it was an apple. So why wasn't it called, say, the Pear of Knowledge or the Banana of Good and Evil? Arguably because the Latin word *malum* means both "evil" and "apple."

In this classic parable, Adam and Eve pick fruit from the tree of life—the one thing God told Adam not to do. Symbolic of earthly knowledge, the tree of life makes the couple self-aware of their bodies and the world outside the idyllic Garden of Eden. They are kicked out of the beautiful garden and the gate is guarded by "the great winged creatures" which are later referred to as *cherubim*.

> **def•i•ni•tion**
>
> **Cherubim** are a group of high-ranking angels. The singular version is cherub.

Cleansing Isaiah's Soul (Isaiah 6:2)

In the year of King Uzziah's death I saw the Lord seated on a high and lofty throne. His train filled the sanctuary / Above him stood seraphs, each one with six wings: two to cover its face, two to cover its feet and two for flying / And they were shouting these words to each other: "Holy, holy, holy is Yahweh Sabaoth! His glory fills the whole earth!" / The door posts shook at the sound of their shouting, and the Temple was full of smoke / Then I said "Woe is me! I am lost, for I am a man of unclean lips and I live among a people of unclean lips, and my eyes have seen the King, Yahweh Sabaoth" / Then one of the seraphs flew to me, holding in its hand a live coal which it had taken from the altar with a pair of tongs / With this it touched my mouth and said, "Look, this has touched your lips, your guilt has been removed and your wrongdoing forgiven." (Isaiah 6:1–7)

A seraph ("burning one" in Hebrew) is a high-level angel, a multiwinged protector of God's throne. Multiple seraphs are called *seraphim*. Isaiah's vision is their first and only direct mention in the Bible, though there are hints of the seraphs' continued presence in the book and additional direct mentions in the Dead Sea Scrolls and other related documents.

The symbolism is powerful here: a seraph puts a hot coal on the prophet's mouth, yet Isaiah says nothing about pain. What is being burned away isn't his skin, but his wrongdoing.

An Angel Helps Jesus' Parents Stay Together (Matthew 1:20)

This is how Jesus Christ came to be born. His mother Mary was betrothed to Joseph, but before they came to live together, she was found to be with child through the Holy Spirit / Her husband Joseph, being an upright man and wanting to spare her disgrace, decided to divorce her informally / He had made up his mind to do this when suddenly the angel of the Lord appeared to him in a dream and said, "Joseph, son of David, do not be afraid to take Mary home as your wife, because she has conceived what is in her by the Holy Spirit / She will give birth to a son and you must name him Jesus because he is the one who is to save his people from their sins." … When Joseph woke up he did what the angel of the Lord had told him to do: He took his wife to his home / He had not had intercourse with her when she gave birth to a son, and he named him Jesus. (Matthew 1:18–25)

The New Testament begins with the birth of Jesus. The famed miracle pregnancy almost broke up Mary and Joseph—not surprising considering they hadn't yet consummated their marriage—but an angel visited Joseph and gave him a message about their future.

An Angel Visits (Acts 10:3)

One of the centurions of the Italica cohort stationed in Caesarea was called Cornelius / He and the whole of his household were devout and pious, and he gave generously to Jewish causes and prayed constantly to God / One day at about the ninth hour he had a vision in which he distinctly saw the angel of God come into his house and call out to him, "Cornelius!" / He stared at the vision in terror and exclaimed, "What is it, Lord?" The angel answered, "Your prayers and charitable gifts have been accepted by God / Now you must send some men to Jaffa and fetch a man called Simon, known as Peter / Who is lodging with Simon the tanner whose house is by the sea" / When the angel who said this had gone, Cornelius called two of the slaves and a devout soldier of his staff, told them all that had happened, and sent them off to Jaffa. (Acts 10:1–8)

The angels visited several major prophets and leaders in the Bible, and Cornelius had a prototypical experience: a visit with a direct message or command from God. However, as we discuss later in this book, no divine message from God is necessary to call in the angels—we can call on them whenever we are in need. The angels can visit several ways, including by sight and sound. We explain the different forms of communication in Chapter 7.

The Angels Save Peter from Jail and Possible Execution (Acts 12:7)

All the time Peter was under guard, the church prayed to God for him unremittingly / On the night before Herod was to try him, Peter was sleeping between two soldiers, fastened with two chains, while guards kept watch at the main entrance of the prison / Then suddenly an angel of the Lord stood there and the cell was filled with light. He tapped Peter on the side and woke him. "Get up!" he said, "Hurry!"—and the chains fell from his hands / The angel then said, "Put on your belt and sandals." After he had done this, the angel next said, "Wrap your cloak round you and follow me" / He followed him out, but had no idea that what the angel did was all happening in reality; he thought he was see-ing a vision / They passed through the first guard post and then the second and reached the iron gate leading to the city. This opened of its own accord; they went through it and had walked the whole length of one street when suddenly the angel left him / It was only then that Peter came to himself. And he said, "Now I know it is all true. The Lord really did send his angel and save me from Herod and from all that the Jewish people were expecting." (Acts 12:5–11)

Unlike humans, the angels are not restricted by time, space, and other basic physical limitations. On God's orders, the angel saved Peter from prosecution. Later in this chapter, when Mary tells the townspeople that Peter is out of prison, they don't believe he could have survived the ordeal alone. They shout, "It must be his angel!"

Archangel Raphael Comes in Disguise to Heal Tobit (Tobit 12:15)

"I am Raphael, one of the seven holy angels, which present the prayers of the saints, and which go in and out before the glory of the Holy One … Now therefore give God thanks: for I go up to him that sent me; but write all things which are done in a book" / And when they arose, they saw him no more / Then they confessed the great and won-derful works of God, and how the angel of the Lord had appeared unto them. (Tobit 12:15–22)

Known as the healer of the Archangels, Archangel Raphael visited Tobit and his son Tobias. Tobit went blind in a freak accident and he sent Tobias out for help. Archangel Raphael actually joined Tobias on the journey, disguised as a fellow Israelite traveler. With Archangel Raphael's help, Tobias helped his father and, after revealing his identity, Archangel Raphael healed Tobit's eyesight.

Archangel Michael Goes to Battle (Revelations 12:7)

"Then a second sign appeared in the sky: there was a huge red dragon with seven heads and ten horns, and each of the seven heads crowned with a coronet ... And now war broke out in heaven, when Michael with his angels attacked the dragon ..." (Revelations 12:3–7)

def•i•ni•tion

Apocalypse is a prophecy of an end-all war or disaster. It can also mean the event itself.

As the last book of the Bible, Revelations is the vision of the earth's *apocalypse:* the beginning of the end. The dragon represents evil, and there is no better angel than Archangel Michael, warrior for good, to battle darkness.

The Archangel rounded up his band of angel warriors and dispatched the fire-breathing monster and its army in one verse. Considering it is against the usual loquaciousness of the Bible's authors, we can assume this one was a quick battle.

Who Are the Archangels?

As shown in the Bible, the Archangels are the superstars of the angelic Universe—well, at least when it comes to us knowing who they are. Many people see the angels as nameless beings helping us along in life, but even the least aware humans have heard of the Archangels, particularly Archangel Michael and Archangel Gabriel, the marquee stars in our ancient as well as modern pop cultures. The other two most well-known are Archangel Raphael and Archangel Uriel. And don't think these are the only Archangels—there are way too many to mention in this chapter.

All angels are special, but the Archangels are certainly extraordinary even among the beautiful angelic choir roaming the earth and beyond.

The Archangels have several specific goals, among them …

- ◆ Angel management.
- ◆ World peace.
- ◆ Globetrotting.

Angel Management

The angels often get lumped together, particularly in pop culture, but there is a definitive hierarchy—after all, a bunch of angels roaming around independently wouldn't get anything done!

If the spiritual world were a business, the Archangels would be the office organizers—helping the work move smoothly and efficiently, dispatching people as necessary, conveying knowledge from the higher up, and stepping in when a challenge is too large for the regular employees.

Perhaps more than any other angels, the Archangels are closest to the will of God. They are considered God's most important messengers.

World Peace

Here on Earth, everyone from politicians to beauty pageant contestants say that their goal is to create world peace. As spiritual beings, the Archangels have the power and the will to make it happen.

However, their main goal isn't to do it themselves, but to motivate *us humans* to create a peaceful world here on Earth. The Archangels use gentle—or, depending on its personality, assertive—persuasion to get us started in the right direction or to keep us on track.

The Archangels specialize in creating *paradigm* shifts, those definitive moments in our life where there is a "before" and an "after." Those growth opportunities open up our eyes to new possibilities

def•i•ni•tion

Paradigm is a framework of ideas or rules people work within. A paradigm shift is a major occurrence that shifts these ideas or rules.

in such a way that we cannot go back to our previous way of thinking. However, as with all angels, they will not help adjust your life without you asking in some form.

Globetrotting

Starvation. War. Poverty. There always seems to be a crisis or challenge and people around the world who are having a more difficult time than we are with our lives. As a result, we may feel guilty about "taking" the Archangels' attention away from others in need.

The truth, though, is that the Archangels never take away from one to give to another. The Archangels are not restricted by time and space, so they have the ability to support, help, and love multiple people all at the same time. Their love is infinite.

The Archangels

They are not human, but the seven Archangels vastly differ in personality and purpose:

- ◆ Archangel Michael—the Defender and Protector. Michael helps inspire courage, bravery, and strength, and protects the weak.

- ◆ Archangel Gabriel—the Messenger. Gabriel communicates love from the higher power, delivering inner peace.

- ◆ Archangel Raphael—the Healer. Raphael heals both humans and animals from addictions and ill health.

- ◆ Archangel Uriel—the Philanthropist. Uriel aids people surviving a crisis of the heart, mind, or body, and helps solve seemingly insurmountable problems and setbacks.

- ◆ Archangel Chamuel—the Compassionate Heart. Chamuel gives people the power to forgive, to forge strong relationships, and to let go of bitterness with love.

- ◆ Archangel Jophiel—the Illuminator. Jophiel helps one keep an open mind, constantly pursuing wisdom and growth.

♦ Archangel Zadkiel—the Diplomat. Zadkiel provides objectivity, allowing people to be less petty and to understand their connection to others and the rest of the Universe.

Let's take a closer look.

Archangel Michael

His service: To serve and protect Earth and the beings upon it.

Archangel Michael is by far the most well-known Archangel and is considered to be the greatest of all the angels by Christianity, Judaism, and Islam. A tall and powerful spirit, his goal is to inspire courage, bravery, and strength in people. His main adversary is fear.

Archangel Michael's name literally means "He who is like God," so you know this angel is all about business. A passionate warrior for good and for God, Archangel Michael is usually depicted armored in classic medieval suiting and carrying a long sword. This does not necessarily indicate violence. In classic iconography, swords symbolize the power of knowledge and the ability to cut away distracting negative emotions to find the real truth. His purpose is to serve as an escort or a courier, helping us to navigate our fears and reconnect to the essence of God.

Beyond inspiring others, Archangel Michael serves as a protector when we are too weak and unable to protect ourselves. On his back is a royal blue cloak, a physical representation of his protective nature. He is often described as a strong, strikingly handsome young man, with chiseled, muscular features and eyes like pools of fire. In the Bible, his skin is described as the "color of copper which radiates and glows from being in the Presence of God."

Archangel Michael is associated with honesty, truth, and the authentic self. He guides you to understand who you really are and humbly serves as a spark of light direct from God. He

Angels 101

Archangels are almost always depicted as young men—perhaps because of their virility and strength—but remember they have never been human! They are pure spirit energy and are several millennia "old."

empowers us with the truth to know our highest self and spirit as well as, perhaps most importantly, to acknowledge our dark side to be free from it.

Archangel Michael understands both darkness and light, so he specializes in bringing lost souls back to God. However, for Archangel Michael, it isn't about judgment, as he understands and wants us to accept both the good and bad within our lives. By accepting our inner conflict, we can better forgive ourselves and others for sometimes falling short of good intentions.

Archangel Michael encourages people to …

- ◆ Find a purpose and take action.

- ◆ Be honest and courageous.

- ◆ Set boundaries.

- ◆ Find or rediscover faith.

- ◆ Be decisive.

Archangel Michael is associated with the color royal blue and the direction south.

Archangel Gabriel

His service: To offer guidance in one's life and mission, assisting in purifying negative emotions and beliefs.

The spiritual leader among the Archangels, Archangel Gabriel has a name that means "God is my strength." Archangel Gabriel helps people find and maintain faith, particularly in our darkest hour. He reminds us that God is ever present. It is as if he wraps those that call on him in a white blanket of purity that heals and comforts.

Archangel Gabriel is the angel of fertility, blessing us with the ability to give life. However, the birth—or rebirth—need not be literal, as Archangel Gabriel not only represents the pregnancy and conception of new beings, but the fertilization and conception of new ideas and trains of thought. The Archangels can help create a spiritual rebirth or, on a more mundane level, a reopening of communication lines between people. Archangel Gabriel's symbolic rebirth also represents a renewal of innocence and a letting go of bitterness from the past.

Communicating clearly and having faith are the keys to humans creating world peace—the main agenda for all Archangels—and Archangel Gabriel helps facilitate communication of all forms. Serving as a sort of muse, Archangel Gabriel can be called upon to give inspiration and to help create the connection between you and your motivation— essentially opening up the communication channels between you and God.

Positive *synchronicity* is also Gabriel's domain. A chance meeting that changes your life, a "misplaced" word that creates a positive dialogue, or a coincidental event that removes roadblocks can happen when you call on Archangel Gabriel. It is in those funny moments in life when God seems to be winking at you.

def•i•ni•tion

Synchronicity is when two seemingly separate events work in conjunction with each other. The results are usually positive.

Archangel Gabriel is an angel of comfort. Pure of spirit, Archangel Gabriel eliminates negative emotions and creates a powerful air of calmness wherever he is present.

Archangel Gabriel encourages people to …

◆ Find a spiritual path.

◆ Create a life plan and purpose.

◆ Build discipline and order.

◆ Overcome discouragement.

◆ Open lines of communication.

◆ Find innocence again.

Archangel Gabriel is associated with the color white and the direction west.

Archangel Raphael

His service: To heal the earth and all upon it.

Archangel Raphael means "God heals," and the Archangel lives up to his name by promoting health, wealth, and balance among humans. He represents inner as well as outer balance, as his providence includes harmful addictions and unhealthy cravings.

It is often assumed that an angel's intention is to sweep in and save us from harm, and even though an angel will protect us, often the primary goal is to empower us to save ourselves. Archangel Raphael is no exception: the Archangel teaches us that we can cure ourselves of addiction, ill health, and negativity with the God-given power we already carry inside. God does heal, but Archangel Raphael teaches that healing comes from within, not from others.

Archangel Raphael's healing knowledge isn't limited to humans, as the Archangel also helps protect and love animals of all kinds. In Hebrew, *Rapha* means doctor or healer.

The Archangel protects and serves all the major earthbound healers, including doctors, veterinarians, and holistic practitioners. Archangel Raphael is also a patron of scientific arts such as math and medicine, which makes sense because logic and empirical systems are just as necessary as faith to heal here on Earth. Ultimately, he represents both heart and mind.

Enlightenments

Archangel Raphael is also the Archangel of travel. He is the one to thank for a safe and peaceful journey.

Archangel Raphael is an angel of balance. He knows the connection between balance and inner peace, and encourages equilibrium between mind, body, and soul.

Archangel Raphael encourages people to …

- ◆ Heal and renew their body, mind, soul, and spirit.
- ◆ Study science, music, and other logical disciplines.
- ◆ Build bridges between enemies.

- Protect themselves.
- Create a balanced life.

Archangel Raphael is associated with the color emerald green and the direction east.

Archangel Uriel

His service: To create peace and soothe conflict.

Archangel Uriel goes by the name "God's Light" and represents *philanthropy*, promoting and teaching love for fellow man. Uriel also means "Fire of God." Fire is traditionally associated with evolution and powerful knowledge.

Philanthropy is often interpreted as a Bill Gates or a Warren Buffett–level person unloading millions of charity dollars, which, for the most part, won't be missed from his billion-dollar bank accounts. However, we need not give money, as we may be rich in knowledge, wise from life, or overflowing with love. Archangel Uriel teaches us to spread whatever we have to those in need. Through Archangel Uriel, we remember that most of the world's problems can be solved if everyone gave what they could— and that true happiness is only found in those who help others.

def•i•ni•tion

Philanthropy can mean goodwill toward others or literally giving a gift or contribution to someone in need.

It's no coincidence that Archangel Uriel helps us understand the material world better. Of course, your clothes and your home are necessary to protect you from harm, but getting a larger television usually does not encourage your spiritual growth. Using wise eyes, Uriel helps us separate the necessary from the superficial.

Archangel Uriel is an angel of service. He knows that service to others is what brings true richness, true rewards, and true inner peace.

Archangel Uriel encourages people to …

- Create peace with others.
- Humbly serve fellow brothers and sisters.

◆ See beyond the material world.

◆ Be loyal to worthwhile causes.

Archangel Uriel is associated with the color ruby red and the direction north.

Archangel Chamuel

His service: To develop a conscious sense of gratitude to the Source and to expand the love in one's heart to include others.

Before world peace can be achieved, people must have the ability to relate to others' unique situations. Archangel Chamuel's name means "He who sees God," and this Archangel helps people see the god, or the higher self, in all people—even their worst enemy. Archangel Chamuel is also the angel of loving oneself, as your worst enemy could be yourself!

On a microcosm level, Archangel Chamuel can help facilitate the connection between two individuals, whether they are in a business, political, or romantic relationship. He is the champion of soulmates— two individuals who are destined to be together—and will help create opportunities for them to meet and stay connected.

Archangel Chamuel is an angel of empathy. Calmness and strength can only come when you are able to put yourself in someone else's shoes. Archangel Chamuel helps us understand empathy and release the emotions that lay heavy in our hearts.

Archangel Chamuel encourages people to …

◆ Heal damaged relationships.

◆ Create new friendships and relationships.

◆ Navigate misunderstandings and miscommunications.

◆ Rise above petty arguments.

◆ Love unconditionally.

Archangel Chamuel is associated with the color pink.

Archangel Jophiel

His service: To understand a higher truth and to bring higher purpose and creativity to your life.

The saying "The more I learned, the more I realized I didn't know" could be an axiom of Archangel Jophiel. He is the ultimate professor of life, teaching people to be open-minded and wise in their decisions. He inspires both teachers and students. Archangel Jophiel can be called for not just traditional teachers and students such as professors and school-children, but for anyone in a mentor or mentee situation.

With a name meaning "Beauty of God," Archangel Jophiel also helps artists looking for their creative inspiration. God's awesome work is all around, but it requires a sensitive, unjaded eye to recognize it. The Archangel helps us let go of the unnecessary past and anything else that might block our creative or spiritual growth.

The Archangel Jophiel is an angel of discovery. Archangel Jophiel encourages us to continue growing and learning, cultivating the desire to live and learn with each new day. *Epiphanies* are his forte.

def•i•ni•tion _____

Epiphany is a seemingly sudden insight that changes one's understanding about life or a specific situation.

Archangel Jophiel encourages people to …

◆ Learn from the past.

◆ Open their minds to new ways of thinking.

◆ Seek spiritual enlightenment.

◆ Heal the planet.

◆ Better understand oneself.

Archangel Jophiel is associated with the color golden yellow.

Archangel Zadkiel

His service: To dissolve and transmute lower energies and to help humankind find forgiveness, diplomacy, and tolerance.

Zadkiel, or "Righteousness of God," is the diplomatic Archangel. Every relationship requires taking and giving, loss and gain, and sacrifice and benefit. Zadkiel teaches us to respect the ebb and flow of relationships and that a short-term loss for oneself may be worthwhile for a long-term gain for all.

To value humanity, however, one must first value individuals, and Zadkiel inspires us to respect our brothers and sisters no matter how different or radical their views may seem. We are all connected in God's love. When that is realized, it is much easier to be tolerant and diplomatic.

Archangel Zadkiel is an angel of focus—focus on the big picture. It's not about sweating the small stuff, and we're all human, no matter how different we seem on the outside. We all need love and we all need to be connected, particularly if world peace is going to be achieved.

Archangel Zadkiel encourages people to …

◆ Be tolerant of differences.

◆ Not be petty or vindictive.

◆ Cultivate unity between different creeds.

◆ Do what is best for the whole, not just the self.

Archangel Zadkiel is associated with the color violet.

The Least You Need to Know

◆ The angels are first mentioned in Genesis as guardians of Eden.

◆ The angels visit prophets in a variety of ways, though they are usually delivering a message from God.

◆ Seraphim and cherubim are high-level angels that appear occasionally in the Bible.

- The Archangels are the organizers of the other angels on Earth.

- There are countless Archangels, but seven are the most well-known. Each has a different purpose.

Chapter 4

Meet the Spiritual Support Team

In This Chapter

- What is the Spiritual Support Team?

- What makes this group different from the angels?

- How the afterlife connects to loved ones

- How to get to know the spirit guides

- How do you connect with the nature spirits?

For the uninitiated, any spirit having an influence in their lives could be an angel. After all, there are countless angels roaming the earth—why *wouldn't* a spirit be an angel?

However, there are spirits just as helpful and as loving as the angels making a difference in your life.

It's time to meet the Spiritual Support Team.

What Is the Spiritual Support Team?

The angels do quite a bit of work in our lives, but they aren't the only advocates from the spirit world. The Spiritual Support Team is different from the angels but has similar goals.

Who's Who on the Team

There are three groups in the Spiritual Support Team:

- Spirit guides
- Deceased loved ones
- Nature spirits

How Does It Differ from the Angels?

The angels are ancient beings that have never been human. On the other hand, two groups within the Spiritual Support Team—spirit guides and deceased loved ones—actually were human at one time. Nature spirits, however, have always been just that—spirits.

The Purposes of the Team

The Spiritual Support Team would like you to live up to your highest spiritual potential here on Earth:

- Spirit guides serve as wise, seasoned mentors.
- Deceased loved ones guide you as a family member or close friend would.
- Nature spirits help us understand and respect Mother Earth.

When the Team Intervenes

The Spiritual Support Team is there when we call, but, like the angels, rarely intervenes without us letting them in. We must call upon them to get their full-fledged support.

We discuss details on how the different members appear, why they appear, and what to expect later in the chapter.

> **Angels 101** _____
>
> Despite popular perception, talking with spirits is actually a simple, focused experience—no fuzzy recollections, and no "blacking out." It is literally like receiving a message from a friend, clear and concise. It won't be similar to a dream, because you'll remember everything that happened and everything that was said.

Spirit Guides

Spirit guides are perhaps the most commonly referenced version of higher beings in movies, television, and modern pop culture in the sense that, at one time, they were humans just like us. Spirit guides help us get to the next level of achievement, whether it is a higher spiritual understanding, a new artistic accomplishment, or another stage in our career.

Unlike the angels, spirit guides appear only when necessary. Think of them like temporary guardians: they come to you during a specific phase, crisis, or challenge in your life; make sure you are okay; and then leave you better from the visit. We must be open to their presence and invite them into our lives, however, before they can intervene on our behalf and actively work to make our situations better.

Spirit guides respect your free will, so you have complete control over if you want to listen to the message or not. Guidance won't be forced, but they are happy to offer gentle advice and insight, like a wise mentor.

> **Advice from Above** _____
>
> Notice how we didn't put the Spiritual Support Team under the angels category? That's because they aren't the angels! The angels are higher beings guiding you from above. Spirit guides and deceased loved ones are former humans who are helping you on your way. However, their impact and importance are equal to the higher beings.

That's not to say that spirit guides are impersonal. In fact, spirit guides may be the most relatable of all the spirit helpers.

All spirit guides were human at one time, and some might have actually spent time with you in past lifetimes. Because they were human, they have an understanding of the challenges, temptations, and limitations of living here on Earth. They are specifically assigned to those who can benefit the most from their own earthly and spiritual experiences, so your spirit guides are essentially tailor-made to your needs. A woman with a learning disability may get assistance from two spirit guides who lived a long, fruitful life within their own limitations, or a drug-addicted young man may be protected by a spirit guide whose own life was cut short by addiction. They have experienced the beginning, middle, end, and new beginning, and they are here to help you through the process as you need it.

> **Angels 101**
>
> Consider your spirit guide a mentor—a seasoned pro who has already gone through what you are experiencing and, because of knowledge from a higher power, can help equip you with the tools for the obstacles and challenges you will face in the future.

They Come in Many Forms

Although spirit guides used to be human, they appear in a form that is most receptive to you. They can be of any nationality, dress in the fashion of a particular era, and present themselves as they were during their last time on Earth. They have distinct personalities of their own.

Some people perceive their spirit guides as a warm light, its protective glow showing them the way. Others hear their spirit guides, perhaps as a bell ringing in the distance telling them everything will be alright. And they could be as concrete as the image of a person you see. Regardless of delivery, spirit guides are determined to help you when you need it.

Personal History

Spirit guides may seem like long-lost friends. Part of this is because they are very familiar with you: your history, your past lives, your ultimate purpose, and your *spiritual contracts*. There is a certain intimacy with spirit guides, as if they know your path before you even know it.

def•i•ni•tion

Spiritual contracts are agreements you've made with other individuals before coming to Earth to teach, love, and guide each other. For instance, in this life your best friend may help you get organized, while you may help her be more fun and spontaneous. Those roles were already decided and agreed upon by both of you before you were born on Earth. Spiritual contracts can apply to boyfriends, wives, or even your boss. It all depends on the depth of the relationship and karmic connection between you and another individual.

A Spiritual Visit

Spiritual studies can be rewarding, but any growth is hard work! Early in her spiritual teacher work, Cecily became a bit overwhelmed and, frankly, procrastinated taking any further steps in her spiritual development. This wasn't meant to be.

Waking up from an afternoon catnap, Cecily saw a strong and beautiful African tribal woman with a large spear by her side. "Wake up!" she said. "You have a lot of work to do!"

The woman told Cecily that she was one of her spirit guides. She was sent to get her motivated, to get back on course for the work she came on Earth to do. Her name was Nabila.

Nabila said she was a Zambian Priestess and was an expert at motivating others with her strong presence and disciplined energy. Cecily calls her a doting drill sergeant. And to this day, Cecily knows she can call on Nabila for that extra boost when she is feeling complacent or insecure.

Enlightenments

Spiritual teacher Sonia Choquette estimates that the average person has 33 spirit guides throughout a lifetime. They come into our lives as we need them.

As with the angels, spirit guides are more than happy to help you along your path.

Deceased Loved Ones

In some cases, it is actually your deceased loved ones who are helping you on your journey. After all, who would know you better? Some consciously choose to come back to Earth to assist their loved ones.

When a person passes away, he or she is eventually given the opportunity to serve others and expand spiritual awareness. One of the options is to help protect and guide living loved ones they originally left behind at death. Don't be afraid: deceased loved ones are not ghosts! Ghosts are usually harmless earthbound spirits stuck between Earth and the afterlife, while deceased loved ones consciously came back from the afterlife to assist you on your journey.

Unlike the angels, these are not extraordinary spirits—their perspectives, experiences, and personalities are no different than when they were living. When they die, they become beings of light and are no longer trapped by the negativity here on Earth. (Quite a comforting experience, we imagine!) They are then given the choice—the free will—to come back to Earth and assist their loved ones. As spirits, they may choose to present themselves in the highest form, almost as if their best features on Earth have been distilled into one wonderful being. That said, they do not automatically become higher beings such as saints, angels, or *Ascended Masters*.

def•i•ni•tion

The **Ascended Masters** are enlightened spiritual beings who excelled here on Earth and have reconnected with God. As true teachers of humankind, their goal is to raise our spiritual evolution. Examples include Buddha, Kwan Yin, St. Germaine, and Jesus.

Just Like Their Old Selves

Deceased loved ones retain their human personality, so their assistance is just an extension of their role on Earth. Your late Uncle Charlie, who was always an incredible cook, may be worth calling when you're hosting your first Thanksgiving. The opposite is also true: if Chuck had sieves for pockets, don't call him for financial insight.

Aside from being in a higher spiritual climate, deceased loved ones are usually just as they were on Earth. If your cousin Richard was sensitive and warm-hearted, expect him to be as such on his return. If your Aunt Jackie was a practical joker, well, don't expect most of her visits to carry a serious tone.

Similar to spirit guides, deceased loved ones can specialize in helping with specific life challenges or areas of study. If the Archangels are big-picture helpers, deceased loved ones are there to help us work through each lesson that is presented to us.

Advice from Above

The Spiritual Support Team does not act as voyeurs watching your every move. Instead, they come down and help you when you need assisting and then leave you be.

Friendly Visitors

Cecily has had several deceased loved one moments. A few years ago, she was boarding a cab outside a hospital where her mother was admitted. Tears ran down Cecily's face, her mother's rapidly declining health almost being too much to bear. She felt alone. As she wistfully looked out of the cab window, the driver's cell phone rang. The ring tone was her late father's favorite song. The driver happened to let the phone ring, and all the while Cecily sat quietly and smiled—she knew her father made sure she got into the right cab at the right time so she would receive his message. She knew it was his sign from the other side—a sign that he was there with her along the way.

In another instance, Cecily went to bed one evening and saw the face of a deceased male relative. His head was aglow in a vibrant white light. He sent her a message, a vision of a woman hunched over in bed coughing incessantly. The coughing rattled her ears. "Tell my sisters to watch their lungs in the wintertime," he said. In the winter, the first sister was diagnosed with a serious lung ailment, while the following winter the second sister was given the same diagnosis.

Angels 101

Imagine how much effort it could take to make your presence known to someone who does not easily see or sense you. Deceased loved ones often work hard to make their presence known. Be aware of communication signs, as they may be trying to send you a message. They can communicate directly to your spirit, so deceased loved ones may connect to you through gut feelings, scents, visions, and other ways.

They Know You

Aside from familiarity, part of the deceased loved ones' healing power comes from them knowing more about your future. They are sensitive to your past, present, and future, and can help guide you to those learning experiences you need to grow. You don't *have* to listen to these members of the Spiritual Support Team, but based on their wisdom areas, they often know what is best for you.

It also is an opportunity to improve or heal any relationship you had with a loved one while he or she was on Earth. We gain perspective on people after they are gone, and deceased loved ones, basking in the healing energy of God, let go of past grudges and issues plaguing their relationships on Earth. It is natural to regret not connecting with someone while alive, but it is important to understand that there is still hope to strengthen the relationship with his or her spirit.

def•i•ni•tion

A **medium** is a person who professionally communicates with the spirit world. Mediums are often hired to connect the living with the deceased.

Contrary to popular belief, a *medium* isn't always necessary to connect with your deceased loved ones. With the intuitive training outlined in this book, you may also be able to communicate with those who have crossed over. Your deceased loved ones are waiting to connect with you after you open yourself up intuitively and become aware of their messages and signs.

Nature Spirits

From stories handed down from generation to generation to the current upswing in fantasy-type books and movies, few spiritual creatures are as mythologized as nature spirits. In fact, throughout history, we've learned about these entities through plenty of real-life encounters and folklore. They are supportive and happy to help guide us, and tales of their kind can be found worldwide in places as varied as Russia, Ireland, and Great Britain.

Some folklore paint nature spirits as dark, vengeful creatures. They are gentle, but do not necessarily trust humans because of our carelessness toward their Mother Earth. The nature spirits are led by Mother Earth, also known as Gaia.

The Four Elements

Nature spirits represent four basic elements: earth, wind, fire, and water. Each elemental spirit has different characteristics:

- **Earth spirits**—Gnomes, tree spirits, and elves. Earth spirits help keep us grounded and level-headed.

- **Wind spirits**—Referred to as sylphs, devas, and fairies. Wind spirits help us use and trust our intuition.

- **Fire spirits**—Known as salamanders. Fire spirits help us get inspired.

- **Water spirits**—Categorized as sprites, undines, and sea nymphs. Water spirits help us renew and rejuvenate our spirit.

As with other members of the Spiritual Support Team, nature spirits can communicate to you in nontraditional ways. Ever feel down and then feel uplifted by a sudden, unexpected whiff of delicate roses? This is a "hello" from the nature spirits.

Although nature spirits are not restricted to our physical limitations, they are still not angels. They are part of the elemental realm, not the angelic one.

Enlightenments

Sixteenth-century Swiss philosopher and alchemist Paracelsus is credited for coining the term *elemental*. The well-respected scientist studied nature spirits and concluded that elemental realms were not fairy tales, but grounded in truth. To this day, he is considered the forefather of all modern-day researchers, writers, and clairvoyants who study and work with nature spirits.

Connecting with Nature Spirits

Nature spirits are one with our environment, so their relationship with humans is rather complex. On one hand, they are part of the support system that wants to help us prosper. On the other hand, it is difficult for nature spirits to watch as we treat our shared Earth less than honorably by excessive pollution, unnecessary waste, and rapidly depleting its scarce resources.

Want to connect with the nature spirits? You have to treat yourself and your environment with as much respect as possible. This means having respect for the earth by recycling, not littering, and helping preserve nature and wildlife as much as possible—in short, leading an ecologically friendly life, honoring the gifts of the earth, and not taking them for granted.

Nature spirits are naturally drawn to pomp and circumstance—joyous ceremonies, fun dances, and celebratory songs. They are drawn to happy children, too. And although they can be found in the city as well as the country, nature spirits are most common in wild, underdeveloped areas where nature itself is uninhibited. They love flowers, but are most drawn to willow trees and daisies.

Healers and *seers* see them more, simply because their insight makes the nature spirits' realm—that is, the elemental realm—as plain as day. Children have an easier time connecting and communicating with nature spirits, too, perhaps because of their innate innocence, unbridled faith, and lack of cynicism.

def•i•ni•tion

A **seer** is a person who can see things other people cannot see easily, such as spirits or even the future.

However, we need not have a gifted third eye nor be a child to bond with the spirits. We can connect easier with the nature spirits by just trying to live at peace with our environment as well as with ourselves.

Bearing Gifts

Most nature spirits find humans intriguing and, as a result, are inclined to give us gifts. They could be tangible items such as flowers, stones, or shells that seem to appear out of thin air; or more ethereal gifts, such as surprising prosperity or positive synchronicity.

The biggest gift they have to offer? The gift of joy. Nature spirits work hard to help us see the positive and feel good about life. They facilitate creativity, renewed innocence, open-mindedness, and wonderment. In short, they make us feel like children again.

Nature spirits also have a natural bond with animals, including pets. You can call on a nature spirit to help your pet or assist you in communicating with your beloved animal. Nature spirits are protectors of wild animals as well.

Enlightenments

Many modern communities actively seek the support of nature spirits. For instance, in northern Scotland, the Findhorn Community has spent decades working with nature spirits. In the early 1960s, community member Dorothy McLean was inspired to apply her meditation practices to communicating with nature. Fellow members and mediators Eileen and Peter Caddy joined in, realizing that with discipline, effort, and respect, they could work with nature on a higher plane. The community soon found its vegetables growing unusually robust and flowers coming in full bloom—well after their natural season. The Findhorn Community is still active and prosperous today.

Spiritual teacher Sonia Choquette says, "The earth is an incredible living, breathing spirit, majestically supporting all of the life on this planet." If Mother Earth is giving life, nature spirits are helping it thrive.

The Least You Need to Know

◆ The Spiritual Support Team of spirit guides, deceased loved ones, and nature spirits are not angels, but assistants in your life's journey.

◆ The Spiritual Support Team knows your history, your life, and most importantly where you are going in the future.

◆ Spirit guides were human and consciously chose to come back to Earth to help you and others.

◆ Deceased loved ones are not ghosts, but spirits interested in helping you in specific situations.

◆ Nature spirits work to protect the environment and represent the four main elements: earth, wind, fire, and water.

Part 2

Angel Messages

Now it's time to start communicating! Part 2 teaches the techniques necessary to connect with the angels and recommends ways to bring their energy more into your life. The spiritual realm can be confusing, so we also provide ways to discern between real angelic guidance and false communication. In this part, you also learn about the language of the angels.

Chapter 5

Brightening Your Light

In This Chapter

- ◆ Raising your consciousness to connect with the angels
- ◆ The seven chakras and auras
- ◆ Understanding the power of thoughts and words
- ◆ Balancing your energy
- ◆ Healing through positive vibrations
- ◆ The life-sustaining energy we get from plants

The angels are more than happy to help us, providing guidance, love, and support. However, their influence becomes much more powerful when we take care of ourselves spiritually and strive to raise our consciousness to connect with them.

Everything Is Energy

Believe it or not, humans actually share something with the angels—we are all composed of energy. That is, we are made of light. In fact, we can connect with the angelic realm because we are made of energy just as they are. We are all born with our energy—our light—at full beam.

Enlightenments

Hawaiian author Koko Willis passes down a beautiful children's parable in *Tales from the Night Rainbow* by Pali Jae Lee (*HO'OPONO* Mountain View, HI Island Moonlight Publishing, 2006). Here is the message from the parable, paraphrased here:

At birth each child is born with a bowl of light. If he tends to his light, he can do great things. Yet, if the child dwells on what he does not have and spreads negativity, the child must drop a stone in the bowl. With each stone the light goes out little by little. Once there are more stones than light in the bowl, the child himself turns to stone without the ability to grow and be of service to others. But, if the child tires of being a stone, all he needs to do is turn the bowl upside down. The stones will scatter and the light will return. The child's light will shine again in the world and he or she will continue to grow once more.

Earth can be harsh, though, and although our lights shine brightly at birth, our doubtful thoughts, difficult experiences, conflicting beliefs, and rough environments can dim our radiance. This lessens our light quotient—which is technically called our energetic vibration—and hampers our ability to connect to the angels.

Highly spiritual beings, the angels are so illuminated with light that they vibrate too quickly for us to see, feel, hear, or connect with them. The angels must slow their vibration as a person raises theirs to connect and communicate—we, in short, have to meet them halfway. If we want to successfully connect with the angelic realm, we must work on brightening our light!

You might say light is actually another name for the life force energy that the Universe is composed of. Energy is the essence of all existence and the fundamental building block of the Universe. It is this living vibrational energy that sustains life and is the connective flow to God. Life force energy has many names: the Chinese refer to the life force as *chi* or *qi*. Hindus call it *prana*. Greeks know it as *pneuma*. Japanese refer to it as *ki*, and the Polynesians call it *mana*.

The Chakras: Human Energy Centers

When the field of energy that surrounds us is vital and strong, we are better able to connect with the angelic realm. Within our own energy fields we have energy centers, or *chakras*, which act as valves for life force energy or chi (*chee*) to flow in, around, and through our bodies. Chi rises from the base of the spine up through the chakras into the head center.

There are seven of these energy centers in the *aura* that spin in a clockwise direction when healthy:

1. Root chakra

2. Sacral chakra

3. Solar plexus chakra

4. Heart chakra

5. Throat chakra

6. Third eye chakra

7. Crown chakra

The speed they spin is based on their position—the higher they are, the faster they spin. Each emanates a different color in the aura.

def•i•ni•tion

A Sanskrit word meaning "spinning wheel," a **chakra** is an energy center located in the larger field of energy around our bodies. Each of the seven chakras runs along the spine and affects our emotional, physical, spiritual, and mental states. An **aura** is the seven subtle bodies, or layers, around the physical body. Each of the subtle bodies works as a team with the chakras to create our own personal energy field. Its condition and radiance reflects our overall health and well-being.

Chakras connect our physical bodies to our higher consciousness. The chakra system is associated with our physical, mental, emotional, and spiritual states. Each chakra relates to specific body organs or systems, as well as emotional and psychological issues.

Changes in our personal flow of energy can understimulate or over-stimulate individual chakras.

Understimulation comes from blockages in the flow of energy through the chakra. There are varying levels of understimulation, from small blockages to a complete block of energy flowing in and out of the chakra. Blockages are created by dense energy created through imbalances such as negative thoughts, feelings, and vibrations in our environment.

Overstimulation comes from too much energy flowing into any one chakra, which creates an imbalance in the whole chakra system. When one chakra has too much energy, it takes away energy from the other chakras. Overstimulation is created through obsessions, compulsions, and addictions to the qualities found in a particular chakra.

First (Root) Chakra

The first chakra, the root, is located at the base of the spine and is associated with basic survival, security, grounding, and self-preservation. The first chakra is the foundation of the whole chakra system and is concerned with physical identity. This chakra emanates a red energy.

- Characteristics of overstimulation include monotony, materialism, and greed.

- Characteristics of understimulation include frequent fear, restlessness, spaciness, and poverty consciousness.

- Part of the body: prostate gland (men), bladder, elimination system, lymph system, skeletal system, teeth, adrenal glands, and lower extremities.

- Healing vocal tone: E as in *Eh*.

Second (Sacral) Chakra

The second chakra, the sacral, is located in the lower pelvis and is associated with base emotion, desire, gratification, and sexuality. The second chakra is concerned with feelings and nurturance of self. This chakra emanates an orange energy.

- Characteristics of overstimulation include being overly emotional, having poor boundaries, addictiveness, and hypersexuality.

- Characteristics of understimulation include frigidity, emotional numbness, and rigidity.

- Part of the body: lumbar region, reproductive system, and sex organs.

- Healing vocal tone: *Oh.*

Third (Solar Plexus) Chakra

The third chakra, the solar plexus, is located in the abdomen center and is associated with strong emotion, ego identity, self-esteem, and motivation. The third chakra is the power center and deals with the projection and perception of self. This chakra emanates a yellow energy.

- Characteristics of overstimulation include being dominating, aggressive, scattered, and overly competitive.

- Characteristics of understimulation include having low self-esteem, passiveness, and a fear of failure.

- Part of the body: solar plexus, large intestines, stomach, liver, muscular system, skin, and pancreas.

- Healing vocal tone: Ahm as in *Ahhh m.*

Fourth (Heart) Chakra

The fourth chakra, the heart, is located in the heart center and is associated with self-acceptance, compassion, love, and forgiveness. The fourth chakra is concerned with the expression of love and relationships. This chakra emanates a green energy.

- Characteristics of overstimulation include codependency, possessiveness, and jealousy.

- Characteristics of understimulation include loneliness, isolation, lack of empathy, and being overly critical.

◆ Part of the body: heart, circulatory system, lungs, chest, and thymus gland.

◆ Healing vocal tone: Ah as in *Ahhh.*

Fifth (Throat) Chakra

The fifth chakra, the throat, is located in the throat and is associated with communication and creativity. The fifth chakra is energetically connected to full self-expression and our ability to speak truth. This chakra emanates a light blue energy.

◆ Characteristics of overstimulation include excessive talking, bluntness, and an inability to listen.

◆ Characteristics of understimulation include fear of speaking up, inhibition, and being overly serious.

◆ Part of the body: throat, neck, arms, hands, and thyroid.

◆ Healing vocal tone: *Oo* (form mouth in a circle).

Sixth (Third Eye) Chakra

The sixth chakra, the third eye, is located in the center of the forehead and is associated with self-reflection, intuition, insight, and imagination. The sixth chakra gives us the ability to perceive things clearly. This chakra emanates a deep blue energy.

◆ Characteristics of overstimulation include difficulty concentrating, nightmares, and delusions.

◆ Characteristics of understimulation include poor memory, denial, and low intuitive ability.

◆ Part of the body: carotids, temples, forehead, and pituitary gland.

◆ Healing vocal tone: *Mm.*

Seventh (Crown) Chakra

The seventh chakra, the crown, is located at the top of the head and is associated with spiritual connection, higher awareness, and spiritual understanding. The seventh chakra is generally considered to be the chakra of consciousness and enlightenment. This chakra emanates a violet and white energy.

- Characteristics of overstimulation include being overly intellectual, confusion, and spiritual addiction.

- Characteristics of understimulation include apathy, cynicism, and closemindedness.

- Part of the body: brain, the nervous system, and pineal gland.

- Healing vocal tone: *Ee.*

Enlightenments

Kirlian photography refers to a form of photogram made with high voltage that visibly shows life force energy around objects. It is named after Russian inventor Semyon Kirlian, who discovered this phenomenon in 1939.

The Aura: Our Human Energy Field

There are seven subtle bodies, or layers, around the physical body, which create the auric body system (aura). Each of the subtle bodies work as a team with the chakras to create our own personal energy field:

- The first aura, etheric body, is often seen clairvoyantly as a thin, invisible layer surrounding the physical body. This subtle body acts as an energetic reproduction of the physical body and is connected with our physical vitality. This body is composed of a web of lines of light that cross each other. These crossings are called *nadis* in Sanskrit or *meridians* in Chinese medicine. Connected to the root chakra.

- The second aura, emotional body, reflects our feelings. Emotions such as happiness, anger, love, and sorrow are all found here. The emotional body is also linked to our past experiences, desires, and traumas. Connected to the sacral chakra.

- The third aura, mental body, holds our thoughts and mental processes. This subtle body corresponds to the conscious mind, intellect, and logic. Because our beliefs and thoughts shape our lives, the mental body assists in creating our life experiences. Any mental illness is reflected here. Connected to the solar plexus chakra.

- The fourth aura, astral body, is a conduit between our daily reality in the physical world and the spiritual realm. Connected to the heart chakra.

Advice from Above

It's not a typo: both the first and fifth auras are etheric. The first works in conjunction with the second.

- The fifth aura, etheric template body, holds the etheric body in place. You might say it is a perfect energetic model for the etheric body to aspire to. Connected to the throat chakra.

- The sixth aura, celestial body, is where consciousness expresses itself as higher feelings such as Universal love, bliss, and interconnectedness or oneness with everything around us. Connected to the third eye chakra.

- The seventh aura, causal body, is where the higher self communicates with the conscious mind. The expressions at this level come from a more keen spiritual awareness and understanding. It is the most highly developed energy structure of all our energetic systems and vibrates at a very high speed. Connected to the crown chakra.

Even though you reside on the earth plane in a physical existence, your energy systems work to keep you continuously connected to the divine energy of the spiritual plane. Your own energy field is a conduit to energy everywhere. You are literally plugged into the "energy soup" that is the Universe.

The Energy of Thoughts and Words

According to Japanese researcher Masaru Emoto, water is a vibrational energy that has the ability to copy, memorize, and transmit information. Featured in the popular independent movie, *What the Bleep Do We Know?* (2004), Emoto's research on the effects of emotions, words, thoughts, and music on water has recently garnered much attention. His popular book, *The Hidden Messages in Water* (see Appendix E), brings forth the foundations of Emoto's pioneering research and includes several photographs of water crystals influenced and formed by specific types of energetic vibration.

In his research, Emoto discovered that water memorizes the vibration of substances and essentially copies the information. For instance, Emoto exposed water to classical music such as Beethoven's *Pastoral Symphony* and Mozart's *40th Symphony* and the results were well-formed crystals with delicate and beautiful patterns. In contrast, when he exposed water to aggressive heavy metal music, the resulting crystals were fragmented and deformed.

As he continued his experimentation, Emoto thought about what would happen if phrases were written on pieces of paper and then wrapped around bottles of water with the words facing in. He wrote out phrases such as "Thank you" and "You fool." The results of the experiment were astonishing. The water exposed to "Thank you" formed beautiful hexagonal crystals, while water exposed to the saying "You fool" produced fragmented and malformed crystals. As Emoto continued with this same experiment, he found that positive words such as unity, love, and friendship created the most beautiful crystals, whereas negative words always created distorted and unattractive crystals.

After further exploration, Emoto discovered that when two specific words were used together the most stunning crystal was formed. These words are love and gratitude. Emoto now believes that it's gratitude that's been missing in the human equation. He goes so far as to say: love and gratitude are the words that must serve as the guide for the world.

Enlightenments

Something to think about: humans are 70 percent water.

The lesson from these experiments is that the vibrational energy from words, intent, and emotions has the power to positively or negatively affect each of us and the world around us.

Aura Hygiene: Staying in Balance

Have you had a shower today? Did you brush your teeth this morning? You probably answered "yes" to one of these daily habits. Our energy systems also need regular cleanings. Over time chakras can become clogged, understimulated, or overstimulated by negative lifestyle choices. Likewise, when we do not take care of our mind, body, spirit, or emotions the aura will often get leaks, tears, and blockages in the different layers of the subtle body. Environmental factors, repetitive negative thought patterns and beliefs, the "stuffing" of emotions, and poor bodily care all contribute to an unbalanced chakra and *auric* system.

def•i•ni•tion

Auric is anything related to your aura.

Many things can increase or diminish your chi, including:

♦ What you eat and drink

♦ Who you spend time with

- ◆ What thoughts you focus on, positive or negative

- ◆ How you express your emotions

Our goal is to create and maintain balance, creating a free flow of our life force energy and a sense of harmony.

What You Eat

The food and drinks that you consume directly affect your chi. Overcooked, processed, or chemically and hormone-packed foods deplete chi. In today's rushed world, fast food is more popular than ever, yet it takes a major drain on our chi because so many digestive enzymes are required to break the food down. If convenience foods are regularly eaten, it puts an unhealthy burden on our digestive organs and exhausts our energy.

What You Drink

Another chi-stealing culprit is caffeine. Caffeine and other stimulants give us unhealthy energy through adrenaline. When our energy reserve is already depleted, caffeine triggers our pituitary gland to secrete a hormone that tells our adrenal glands to produce adrenaline, putting us into fight or flight mode (the body's automatic physical response to stress, harm, or threat).

Regular caffeine consumption fatigues the adrenal glands and further robs us of chi.

Fortunately, chi can be balanced by making wise food choices.

Chi builders include the following:

- ◆ Organic produce and meats

- ◆ Freshly cooked meals

- ◆ Raw foods

- ◆ Pure water

- ◆ Sprouted grains

◆ Green foods (wheat grass, barley grass, spirulena, chlorella)

◆ Digestive enzyme supplements

Chi stealers include the following:

◆ Alcohol

◆ Fast food

◆ Processed food

◆ Sugary snacks

◆ Coffee

◆ Soda

Nature's Way

Ancient as well as contemporary Hawaiian practices encourage the gathering of mana (or chi) from the natural world around us. The Pacific Islander belief systems say that humans are at one with all things because everything is in fact mana. Out in nature energy is easily absorbed, so it is not difficult to be energized and balanced as it is in the bustling city. Walking near the ocean or a lake, spending time around trees and plants, and hiking in the mountains are all powerful sources of natural energy. Similar to Hawaiians, it is important to take time out of our busy schedules and enjoy the gifts of nature.

Qigong: An Ancient Chinese Art

It would seem like a no brainer that exercise would be beneficial to our flow of chi. This is true—any daily cardio activity will give our circulating chi a jump start. Yet, there is a special group of exercises that work to accumulate and circulate chi within the body. *Qigong* (*chee gong*) is the ancient Chinese art and science of becoming aware of one's life force energy and learning how to master its flow through a controlled composition of posture, movement, meditation, and breathing. The word means "breath work" or "energy work" in Chinese.

A common practice in China, Qigong has started gaining popularity in both the United States and Europe in recent years because of its simplicity and powerful benefits for everyone. There are techniques suitable for men and women, young and old, athletes and sedentary, and the disabled. Qigong movements are fluid and graceful with a minimum of exertion. Results of this ancient therapeutic system are truly transformational; the most common include enhanced balance, flexibility, coordination, stamina, and a stronger immune system. As a natural complement to *acupuncture*, Qigong is a preventative and self-healing part of Chinese medicine that teaches patients how to improve their own health.

Qigong works as a bridge from physical health to spiritual, emotional, and mental well-being. Qigong philosophy and techniques are mentioned in the *Dao De Jing*, a classic text of Taoist philosophy written in fourth century B.C.E. The Qigong system embodies the Taoist philosophy of gaining expanded consciousness and a true sense of balance through means of little effort or resistance.

def•i•ni•tion

Acupuncture is an ancient form of traditional Chinese medicine that works directly with the flow of chi. It is the practice of inserting thin needles into specific points on the body with the aim of relieving pain or for other therapeutic purposes.

Reiki: Hands-On Japanese Healing

Reiki (*ray key*) is an ancient system of hands-on energy healing. The Japanese word *Reiki* means "Universal life energy." Similar to other healing therapies, Reiki works with balancing and restoring the flow of chi. Based on the oral teaching of Guatama Buddha, Reiki techniques were actually lost for centuries until the late 1800s. They were rediscovered by Mikao Usui, a Japanese Christian minister searching for spiritual healing knowledge. The teachings led Usui to Mount Kurama for a 21-day meditation and fasting. On the last day, Usui had a vision: a flash of light and ancient healing symbols from the heavens. Usui interpreted these symbols and became the first practitioner of the system we now know as Traditional Reiki.

In Reiki, the practitioner transfers energy through his or her hands to balance the client's energy and jump start the body's natural ability to heal. The flow of energy affects your mind, body, emotions, and spirit.

Angels 101

If you decide to make your own pilgrimage to Mount Kurama, realize that it can also be called Mount Koriyama or Mount Kurayama. It's right outside of Tokyo.

Reiki restores vitality by relieving the physical and emotional effects of unreleased stress. It gently and effectively opens blocked energy channels, chakras, and clears the energy bodies, resulting in a feeling of deep relaxation and peacefulness. Reiki is not only a natural form of healing, but is simple to learn and safe to use. It is the perfect complement to any therapeutic practice.

Sound Healing

Scientific studies show that sound can produce changes in our bodies. We are vibrating energy beings, and vibrations create sound waves. Every atom, molecule, cell, gland, and organ of the human body absorbs and gives off sound. We may not perceive the sound, as it may be below or above the threshold of our hearing. When an organ or body part is healthy, it creates a natural sound frequency in harmony with the rest of the body. Disease or health disturbances show up when a body is out of harmony. With disease, the affected part of the body takes on a different and unharmonious sound pattern. Healing with sound has been found to restore harmonic patterns within the body. If that is not enough good news, vibrations have also been known to lower heart rate variability, relax brain wave patterns, and reduce respiratory rates, leading to reduced stress hormones.

Working on the physical level is just half of it—sound is an equal-opportunity healer and is extremely effective on the human energy field, leading to increased emotional and psychological well-being. Sound healing is actually a return to ancient cultural practices that used chants and singing bowls to restore health and balance; Sufis, Hindus, Native Americans, and Catholic monks have long relied on sound to heal. There are various methods of healing with sound such as vocal toning and chanting, emotional releasing, and crystal and Tibetan singing bowls.

Singing Bowls

Since ancient times, singing bowls have been traditionally used throughout Asia as part of Buddhist practice. The customary use for these bowls is as a support for meditation and prayer. Now available worldwide, singing bowls have expanded in function and are found to be a common accompaniment to all types of alternative healing and spiritual practices such as meditation, relaxation practices, health care, and music therapy.

The more common Tibetan or Himalayan singing bowls are crafted from a bronze alloy with copper, tin, zinc, and iron. The biggest producers are Nepal and India.

Enlightenments

In more recent years, crystal singing bowls have gained popularity. Crystal singing bowls are traditionally white frosted bowls made from 99 percent pure crushed quartz. They come in a variety of sizes, ranging from 6 to 24 inches in diameter. The shape and size of the bowl affects the tone. Crystal has the power to amplify, transform, store, and transfer energy. Think of crystal-based electronic devices such as timepieces, microphones, and radio and television equipment.

Singing bowls are played by the friction of rubbing a wooden, plastic, or leather-wrapped mallet around the rim of the bowl to produce overtones and a continuous "singing" sound. Singing bowls may also be played by striking with a soft mallet to produce an incredibly rich and beautiful sound. When a bowl is played in close proximity to the user, a pleasant vibrational or buzzing feeling can be felt throughout the body.

Some doctors are now using singing bowls as a powerful healing complement to Western medicine. For instance, Mitchell L. Gaynor, M.D., director of Medical Oncology and Integrative Medicine at the Strang-Cornell Cancer Prevention Center and author of the book, *Sounds of Healing* (see Appendix E), uses crystal bowls and Tibetan bowls in his practice with cancer patients.

Toning

Although it sounds like a gym routine, toning is the name of a simple and natural form of sound therapy that works directly on the human energetic field. A tone is a distinct sound that maintains a constant pitch and vibration. In the process of toning, single tones—often vowel sounds—are sustained vocally, such as "Aaaah" or "Ooooh."

Think of the popular meditation chant Aum. The high vibratory frequency created by our vocal chords can be both penetrating and therapeutic. Since ancient times, many cultures have used certain tones for healing and release. For instance, Native Americans often use chanting in ceremony.

Toning can be used as a daily practice for relaxing and releasing. Toning is an intuitive practice because it is an innate form of healing and nurturing that we, as humans, all share. Think about a baby cooing. From the time we are born, we use our own sound vibrations to soothe ourselves and seek comfort from others.

Toning pioneer Laurel Elizabeth Keyes writes about this phenomenon in her book, *Toning: The Creative Power of the Voice* (see Appendix E), when she refers to the little cries and murmurings of infants as natural toning. Without adult inhibitions in place, young children emotionally express themselves by crying out, laughing, and screaming. By the time we are adults, however, our emotional responses have become more suppressed through parental and societal conditioning. When these emotions are held in, tensions, pressures, imbalances, and blockages occur in our energetic field and especially in our emotional body. Toning is one of the most powerful tools for pent-up and repressed emotions, because it is able to cleanse the energetic field through vibrations.

> **Advice from Above**
>
> Vibrational healing is a complement to Western medicine and should not be used as a substitute for medication in cases of chronic depression or other psychiatric disorders.

Emotional Release Therapy

A form of toning often used is emotional release therapy. A trained therapist will lead a client through a verbal release of pent-up emotion, such as crying, screaming, or humming for emotional, spiritual, and physical well-being. Intense and high-pitched sounds help break up energetic blockages. This type of healing is often liberating and profound.

Flower Power: The Energy of Plants

Plants provide us with life-sustaining energy every day. All life on Earth depends on the energy given off by plants to stay alive. Through a process called *photosynthesis*, all plant life takes in light energy from the sun and converts it into oxygen and energy-packed nutrients. As a form of vibrational healing, plant energy is regenerating, oxygenating, and purifying.

Flower Essence

Flower essence remedies are water-based infusions of the blossoms from a wide variety of flowers, trees, shrubs, and plants. The essences are vibrational in nature and work deeply within the human energetic field to restore balanced energy flows. Their most significant impact comes from rebalancing and transforming the emotions. These essences encourage a gentle and noninvasive clearing of stuck negative emotions by restoring energy flow and healthy vibratory frequencies in the emotional body.

Flower essences were first developed in the 1930s by Dr. Edward Bach, an English physician and homeopath. In creating the essences, Bach chose to rely on his background in healing and his intuition. Using his sixth sense, Bach discovered therapeutic plants and flowers— eventually creating 38 remedies geared toward a particular mental or emotional state. Willow, for instance, helps users release resentment and violet helps relieve loneliness. Today, Bach Flower Essences are the most widely distributed flower essences, and his blended tonic Rescue Remedy is popular worldwide.

Flower essences can be taken orally or topically. How do they work? When combined with the human energetic field, the high vibrational frequencies of essences gently raise our own frequencies, creating a therapeutic energetic shift.

An essence is the natural energy of a particular plant or flower that's captured and stored for future use. Essences are made by floating the blossoms of the chosen plant on the surface of a bowl of pure spring water and then infusing the water with sunlight for many hours. During this time, the vibrational imprint of the plant's life force energy is transferred to the water. Through Dr. Emoto's experiments with water, described earlier in this chapter, we know that water has the capacity to memorize and store energetic information. When complete, the flower essence is preserved and stored for later therapeutic use.

Aromatherapy

From scented candles to perfumed bath and shower products, aromatherapy has become increasingly popular in America. There is more to it than a pleasant smell, however. Similar to flower essences, aromatherapy works directly with the human energy field through vibrations. The purest and most healing form of aromatherapy is found in therapeutic-grade essential oils. Because of their high, positive vibration, pure essential oils help promote emotional, physical, and spiritual healing.

Angels 101

Look for and purchase only the highest grade oils for aromatherapy. Aromatherapy pioneer Gary Young, the founder and president of Young Living Essential Oils, is recognized in the aromatherapy world as one of the leaders in the cultivation, distillation, and production of organically grown, therapeutic-grade essential oils. He is one of North America's foremost authorities on essential oils and medicinal aromatherapy, and travels the world in search of the finest and purest ingredients. The website for Young Living is www.youngliving.us.

Similar oils date back to ancient times and are some of humankind's first medicine. The production and blending of oils was common in ancient Egypt, and recipes were often recorded on walls in hieroglyphics.

The Least You Need to Know

◆ We must raise our vibrations higher to better match the frequency of the angels to effectively connect with them.

◆ Energy is the essence of all existence and the fundamental building block of the Universe.

◆ Our energetic field is directly impacted by our environment and what we think, eat, and feel.

◆ Many alternative and holistic healing methods can raise our vibration and keep us in balance.

◆ Each chakra relates to specific body organs or systems, as well as emotional and psychological issues.

◆ Plants used in aromatherapy, and flower essences specifically, are natural forms of emotional therapy.

Chapter 6

Inviting the Angels into Your Life

In This Chapter

- ◆ How the angels help and inspire us
- ◆ How the angels keep us out of harm's way
- ◆ Ways the angels can improve your life
- ◆ Six essential steps you need for calling on your angels

Have you ever wished for an entourage of helpers and assistants available to you day or night just like the rich and famous have? It would make life so much easier. The good news is that you already have a group of spiritual helpers surrounding you. They are called the angels, and they are waiting to assist you in every aspect of your life at a moment's notice.

The angels are everywhere, standing by to help each of us. Not only do the angels want to aid us, they delight in it, because their purpose and passion is to be of service to humanity. They are ready and waiting to support us, but will not interfere in our lives without our express permission. You must invite the angels into your daily life to benefit from their many blessings.

The angels are one of our greatest heavenly resources. As long as our desires are aligned with God's will and our individual soul purpose—what you came to Earth to do and to be—the angels will work tirelessly to help us, guide us, and intervene on our behalf. The angels are in service to raise our consciousness, help us with our spiritual growth, keep us on track, and assist us with every aspect of our daily life. When we invite them in, they enhance our lives in many powerful and wondrous ways.

The Angels Make Our Lives Easier

The angels want to make our lives easier. They can help us with anything and everything in our daily lives—big or small. Whenever you find yourself in need of support for anything, it's time to call on the angels and request their assistance.

Big Dreams

Each of us has wishes and dreams in every area of our lives. Yet sometimes we have difficulty turning these desires into reality. Our angels are willing to work around the clock to help us succeed and find happiness in life, so we don't have to struggle so much. Their wise guidance and behind-the-scenes action can support us in realizing the dreams we hold close to our heart. Our angelic helpers are always looking out for our best interests and the best interests of those around us in our work, home life, finances, relationships, and leisure pursuits.

Here are some examples of dreams that the angels can support:

- Creating career opportunities, changes, and advancements
- Finding a soulmate
- Starting a family
- Writing a book
- Meeting new friends

- Creating extra income
- Finding your dream house
- Manifesting travel adventures

Small Tasks

Not only can the angels aid us in realizing our loftiest goals and dreams, but they are also wonderfully adept at assisting us with our smallest daily tasks, such as finding a parking space.

In fact, asking for a parking space is a great way for many to start working with the angels and to see quick results. Because the angels are eager to help us with any ordinary task, they are the best shopping companions, experts at helping find lost objects, and skilled navigators when we are lost or running late.

The angels may be divine beings direct from God, but they are willing and able to offer practical help to us humans.

Here are some examples of ways the angels can assist us (remember, the possibilities are endless!):

- Selling and buying a home
- Picking out gifts for others
- Finding the best deals
- Locating our keys, purse, or wallet
- Arranging travel plans
- Inspiring home design and décor
- Finding good childcare

Advice from Above

The angels will not assist us if our wishes go against God's will and the greater good for everyone involved in a situation. For instance, do not expect help in seeking revenge, teaching someone a lesson, or any form of manipulation.

Looking for Comfort

The angels love each of us unconditionally and are compassionate to our hardships in life. Although these light beings have never been human themselves, they are highly attuned to our pain, frustration, anger, and sorrow and can easily sense when we need emotional support. In our darkest hours, they find ways to provide comfort and soothe our aching hearts. Sometimes it's a sensation of healing warmth and love that spreads from our heads to our toes. Cecily likes to call these "angel hugs." Other times, a loved one might be prompted by his or her own guardian angels to give you the extra support that you need.

One of their favorite ways of comforting us humans is to bring us wisdom from unexpected sources. Have you ever been sad or depressed and a stranger just happened to say the right thing at the right time to make you feel better? Other times, you might have heard something on the radio or on television that rang true for your current situation and brought you solace. These are just two examples of the loving way that the angels assist us.

The Angels Make Our Lives Safer

It might be said that the angels are like our invisible bodyguards. The angels watch over us to keep us out of harm's way. Keeping us safe is one of their most important jobs.

For example, our angels help us while driving by reminding us to pay attention, keeping us awake, and giving us frequent nudges to check our automobiles. Whenever we are in a potentially dangerous situation, our angels are there to help alert us and protect us.

Some years ago, Cecily experienced the warnings of her angels before an intruder broke into her home. For hours she had tried to go to sleep without success. Every time she closed her eyes a prickly sensation would go up her spine and keep her awake, and as a result she was up most of the night. At 4 A.M., Cecily was still awake and heard a thumping noise in her kitchen. A burst of energy was sent her way and she heard the words "make lots of noise" in her ears. Cecily walked toward the kitchen shouting the whole way. She stopped short to see a masked intruder in her kitchen starting to run out the back door. The noise she created had alarmed him so much that he ran out of the house as fast as he could! The next time you experience a near miss or a narrow escape, you can be sure that your angels were on duty.

The Angels Make Our Lives Magical

You don't have to go to a magic show to witness true acts of magic. Pulling a rabbit out of a hat would be considered amateur night when compared to the size and scope of miracles performed every day by the angels. The angels lend a magical touch to everything they do. Most importantly, they work their magic by adding more vibrancy and love to our lives. When these heavenly helpers are working on our behalf, life becomes an awesome adventure.

Through their loving guidance, our eyes are opened to new ways of thinking, being, and relating that benefit us and the world around us. It is by helping us remember our magnificence and wisdom and by showing us how to open our hearts that the angels bring us awareness of the beauty and abundance all around us.

Angels 101

Angel author Terry Lynn Taylor affectionately refers to the angels as "changels" because of their ability to be great catalysts of change. When we invite the angels in, it is important to be willing and ready to see change in our lives.

The Three E's

The angels like to help us by performing the three E's:

- ◆ Encouraging

- ◆ Empowering

- ◆ Educating

They know that each of us was born with a greater purpose—a unique role to play in the world—and they work to keep us on task and fulfill our mission. They are also right there to support us when the chips are down.

It's easy to get discouraged in this sometimes chaotic world. We may have lost a job, a loved one, or our direction in life. We may struggle financially and feel that there is no hope for a brighter future. Most of us will fall off course from time to time, and it is often our angels that gently nudge us to pick up the pieces and get back on track again.

These divine beings often serve as catalysts to positive change in our lives. As with God, the angels can serve as our greatest cheerleaders and encourage us to look for opportunities in life—to turn in directions that are right for us to grow, expand, and succeed.

The angelic realm also knows that many spiritual growth opportunities are disguised as problems. They enjoy giving us the skills and guidance that empowers us instead of simply fixing all our troubles or bailing us out. Our heavenly supporters offer us courage and the ability to take more risks in life, so we can be in alignment with our highest purpose.

One of the most essential roles of the angels is to mentor and educate us in the spiritual workings of the Universe. These amazing teachers open us up to new insights and perceptions of our small world and the infinite Universe around us.

When the angels are invited into our lives, they show us the importance of looking beyond our narrow views and give us a more expanded perspective by lifting the veil that keeps us blinded to our potential. The more we come to understand the world and our place in it, the more we thrive!

Daily Inspiration

You could say that inspiration is equal parts divine guidance and strong motivation shaken and stirred to perfection. It's not hard to imagine that the angels make inspiration an art form. Beauty, joy, *wonder,* creativity, and awe are all forms of inspiration, and the angels are adept at bringing each of these qualities into our lives. At a basic level, inspiration helps us get in touch with the strong creative life force or aliveness moving through us all. In reconnecting us with our innate vibrancy,

def•i•ni•tion

> **Wonder** is when our senses are excited by novelty, astonishment, surprise, or admiration.

the angels assist in uplifting us and generating momentum that fuels our heart's desire. We are stimulated to feel more, do more, and create more when we are bitten by the inspiration bug.

Want the good things in life? All you need to do is notice the gifts already there. There are whole legions of angels who would like to make sure that we notice all the good things going on around us. They delight in reminding us to marvel at the little things in life. Things such as when you are walking down the street and notice a beautiful sunset or a lovely garden, see a peaceful newborn baby, or hear a favorite song on the radio, these are the moments that the angels like to send our way. Life becomes fuller and more joyous when we appreciate the splendor that surrounds us every day.

The angels recognize that joy is contagious and is one of the most powerful ways to connect with the Divine. Life can be too serious, so the angels want us to lighten up, laugh, and get our creative juices flowing. They are happy to help us live more fully in the moment and find our childlike sense of wonder again. The angels remind us that for every petty annoyance in our lives, there is something beautiful or amusing right around the corner.

Bless You!

There is something called an "angel blessing" that many experience each day. Sometimes we recognize these gifts and sometimes we don't, but the angels are always hard at work bestowing these little jewels called blessings on us. Because the angels are messengers directly from God, receiving a blessing is a gift from God. Blessings frequently appear to us in the form of healing, prosperity, triumphs, harmonious relationships, and new beginnings. Others may call examples of these "lucky breaks," but there is no such thing as simple luck when the angels are working with you.

Often these blessings are brought to us through synchronicity. Synchronicities can appear in many ways; a life-changing book falls in front of you in the bookstore, you run into the head of a company you would like to work for, your seat assignment on a plane has you seated next to your future husband or wife, or you get a bit of information right as you need it.

Cecily experienced her own blessing when she first moved to San Diego. She and her husband (then boyfriend), Todd, were looking to rent a reasonably priced home in a beautiful and historic neighborhood that had studio space for his art. The only problem was that this particular neighborhood was known for its high housing costs. Cecily called on the angels to help find the right house at the right price in their desired neighborhood. Within a day, they received a blessing. As they drove into the neighborhood to look around, they saw a "for rent" sign immediately with an affordable rent listed on it. Todd called the number on the sign and the owners mentioned that they just put the sign up and just happened to be at the house and could give them a tour right away. The house included everything on their wish list, including the studio space. Of course, the house was rented to Cecily and Todd that very day!

The Angels Give Our Lives Greater Meaning

The angels are always looking for opportunities to share their Universal wisdom with us. They want us to know that the way we live our lives has a great impact on the Universe around us and that we are given this power for an important purpose—to spread love. Love is the highest vibration and our highest goal. There are two must-have principles that help us better understand the nature of reality and our place in it—interconnectedness and choice.

The Web of Life

Did you ever have a moment in nature where you were so at peace that you felt almost at one with everything around you? You could say that for an instant the illusion of separateness was gone. In truth, everything in the Universe is energetically connected. There exist threads of energy that connect each of us on Earth together, almost like a spider web. No matter how different we all are, on a basic energetic level we all are one. We are all a part of the energy direct from the Source.

Want to see our interconnectedness in action? Have you ever heard of six degrees of separation? Recent studies have shown on a basic level that we are only six people away from any person on the planet.

Researchers Eric Horvitz and Jure Leskovec looked at communication on the Microsoft Messenger instant-messaging network for the month of June 2006 and determined we are in fact all linked by only 6.6 degrees of separation.

It is often said that fear and love is all there is. The angels know this well. When we mistakenly feel that we are separate from this divine energy, we go into a place of fear which ultimately brings us struggle and pain. Yet when we acknowledge and embrace our interconnectedness, we find love and step into the flow of the Universe. The consciousness and awareness of the masses affects each of us on this planet. What affects one affects all in varying degrees. A single thought of love or hate can have ripple effects. Our angels are here to remind us that we have the power to impact the world in a positive way by our actions, thoughts, words, and emotions.

When we unite with others to help with the greater good of humanity, we can do impressive things. Life is not just about what we accomplish or how much money we make. It is about how we can make the world a better place.

Enlightenments

Six degrees of separation is a theory that stems from research done in the United States by Stanley Milgram in 1969 called the "the small world experiment." Milgram took a sample of 64 people and found that the average number of jumps for a letter to travel from Omaha, Nebraska, and Wichita, Kansas, to a target recipient in Boston was 6.2. These findings led to the notion that there are just six degrees separating us from one another.

Deciding Our Path

It is common to blame God or destiny for life's difficulties. The angels know better and want to spread the message that each of us is born with choice and free will. All of us are given the opportunity to choose what we will become, how we will act, and what we will do with our lives. On every level of who we are, conscious and unconscious, personality and soul, we are deciding what path our lives will take.

Within each of us are many choices, and our free will allows us to choose from several options in any given moment. Where we take our vacations, who we spend time with, and where we work are all examples of our free will in play. We are on Earth to learn the lessons our soul needs for growth. Earth is a place of action and reaction. For every choice or action, there is a good, bad, or neutral outcome. For instance, when we make decisions for the greater good, we often have a positive outcome compared to making decisions that will only benefit ourselves.

Good choice or bad choice, God and the angels support us in every decision we make. The angels are sent to help us learn our lessons and grow so we can make better choices the next time.

The Six Essentials for Calling on Our Angels

There is a special six-step formula for calling on our angels that works every time: ask, partner with your angels, trust, release, allow and receive, and say "thank you."

Ask

The angels cannot intrude on our free will, so we must ask them to assist us. You may be as formal or informal as you like when you request their help. These heavenly helpers will answer to a prayer, a thought, or a verbal cry for help in an instant. There is no steadfast rule to call the angels to you, so you can never mess up. Because the angels are messengers directly from God, when we petition an angel for help, we can be rest assured that God has heard our plea. It is God's will for the angels to surround us and aid us whenever we call on them, so don't be afraid to call on them often.

Some might be hesitant to call on the angels for little things, because they feel that they are taking the angels away from something more important. This is not the case. Because there are no boundaries of space and time in the angelic realm, angels can be in many places at once and there is an infinite amount of angelic support available. You can ask for as many angels as you would like to join you. If you feel you need a thousand angels, go ahead and ask.

The sky is the limit when working with these divine beings; anything that you can imagine is worth asking for. The angels want to serve you in the best way possible, so concentrate on what you desire and be direct and detailed in your request. Remember, the grander, the better— be clear when you are looking for a blessing!

Angels 101

Author Doreen Virtue teaches that we can call on the angels on behalf of someone else. Sending an angel blessing to a loved one is an act of love and is not a violation of that person's free will. It is ultimately up to each person whether to listen to the angels' messages and accept their assistance.

Partner with Your Angels

The angels are willing to assist us, but they are not here to do all the work. Although these heavenly helpers delight in making us happy, if we expect them to be like Santa Claus or a genie in a bottle granting us all our wishes, we will be sorely disappointed.

It is not enough just to ask for things; we have to partner with the angels and do our part. For instance, if you want better health, you have to accept responsibility by eating well and exercising. If a romantic partner is what you are seeking, you will need to be out and about and projecting your best self to meet that special someone. The angels can put us on the path to success, but ultimately it is up to us to take the first step.

Another fundamental reason that the angels expect us to share the load is that they recognize the importance of our spiritual evolution. Continually rescuing us, bailing us out, or doing the work for us does not do us any favors in the long run. The angels know that for us to grow, we must learn through our own actions and choices. Although they are happy to guide us and show us the way, they will never interfere with our life lessons.

Trust

We live in a society where we expect everything to happen fast! Many of our day-to-day activities can be completed by the push of a button. What was life like before cell phones, computers, ATMs, and the Internet? A lot of us can't remember. Unlike our technology, the Universe works with a thing called *divine timing*. This type of timing is when all things line up perfectly to give us the result we are looking for. Sometimes this just can't be rushed. When God's timing and our timing do not coincide, we often get impatient, frustrated, and distrustful. The angels don't like to see us suffer, so they are continually guiding us to develop faith and trust in the process.

In cultivating trust, we remember that God and the angels love us unconditionally and always want the best for us. No sincere request or prayer goes unanswered. There is always a grander plan than we can imagine or conceive of that is falling into place piece by piece in front of us.

Our vision is often limited, but the Universe is able to see the big picture and how it all fits together. Know that the angels are busy behind the scenes bringing people and circumstances together at the right time for the best outcome possible.

Release

Have you ever heard the phrase "let go and let God"? Surrendering is an essential part of the process. After we do what we can on our end, the angels want us to release our problems and wishes to them. When we hold on tightly to what we have asked for, our inner control freak is essentially telling the Universe "I need to do it." This type of struggle for control sets up a pervading energy of worry and fear around our request.

It is by realizing that we can do no more and by letting go and letting God and the angels handle the details, the burden is taken off our shoulders. It is then that we can take comfort in the fact that we do not need to know everything and that we have done all we can. The quicker we let go, the quicker we see results.

Allow and Receive

It is a well-known fact that when we get in "the zone" we can do great things. Athletes and successful people around the world say they achieve the most when they enter this Zen-like place. The zone is really a position of allowing and receiving. An important ingredient in getting what we want is allowing ourselves to take in all the goodness the Universe has to offer.

An angel's job is to give us what we need, but we must believe it is our inherent right to accept all the wonderful things that they bring to us. Allowing calls for us to acknowledge that we are deserving and worthy of receiving our desires. This can be difficult for those that struggle with blocks from childhood and feel that they are undeserving of such abundance. When we are unsure, we must look for and be open to the angels' wise guidance to heal our wounds and low self-esteem. The energy of allowing and receiving is smooth, flowing, and easy.

Thank Your Angels

Remember to thank your angels when you receive their assistance. The angels don't need a thank you to do what they do, yet it is an essential step to infuse the loving energy of gratitude into the process. Only when we are grateful for each blessing we receive will we be in the flow to receive other blessings.

The Least You Need to Know

- The angels can assist us with any need, big or small, but we must invite them into our lives for them to help us.

- The angels make our lives easier, safer, and more magical, as well as giving our lives more meaning.

- The angels inspire us to reach our highest potential.

- We must trust and have faith that the angels are always working on behalf of our best interest.

- The six essential steps for calling on your angels are: ask, partner with your angels, trust, release, allow and receive, and say "thank you."

Chapter 7

Communicating with the Angels

In This Chapter

- ◆ Learning about the sixth sense we all possess
- ◆ Ways that the angels send us messages
- ◆ Enhancing our ability to receive angelic guidance
- ◆ Signs that the angels are near
- ◆ Blocks to receiving angelic guidance

After the angels have received our invitation and they are present in our lives, it is time to look for the angelic messages that start to appear. The angels know we have no time in our busy lives to solve complex puzzles or secret codes; communicating with the angels is meant to be simple. Divine messages can come in such simplistic or subtle forms that it is important to learn the language of the angels, so we don't miss them.

The angels do want to connect with us and have various ways to get our attention. Angelic communication is constantly coming to us, but we need to learn to listen and observe to become aware of how our angels impart their guidance to us. The most common ways that the angels communicate with us are through seeing, feeling, hearing, knowing, and experiencing.

Angelic Communication

Communicating with our angels is a natural ability that we all can enjoy. Each of us possesses intuitive gifts that are waiting to be tapped. Cecily's spiritual teacher, Sonia Choquette, says that we're all spiritual beings endowed with six, not five senses, and the sixth sense is all-knowing intuition. Most of the time we relate to the world with our basic five senses, but when communicating with the angels we often need to open our sixth sense to perceive their many forms of making contact. When our sixth sense is being flexed and used, our intuitive abilities can help us experience essential types of angelic guidance—visual, aural, emotional, and insightful communication.

Visual Communication: Seeing Messages

Clairvoyance (clear seeing) is one means of angelic communication. You may receive divine guidance through images, visions, and mini movies that play in your mind or within your field of vision. Visions are most often in full color, but can also be in black and white. Many times the images that you receive are reminiscent of daydreams, yet they are more vivid or animated. Cecily has seen all types of clairvoyant movies. Some have reminded her of watching an old silent film; others have been more like a Disney cartoon!

When using the gift of clairvoyance, our third eye chakra (see Chapter 5 for more on the chakras) works in conjunction with the occipital lobe of our brain to let us see beyond the veil. Communication can be in the form of pictures, signs, letters, colors, and sparkles of light. These scenes are oftentimes symbolic, but the meaning is usually very clear to the recipient. The angels work with our personal knowledge base and perspective to send us a visual message that we can understand. For instance, when Cecily sees a small child playing in her mind's eye, she recognizes this image as a symbol for being playful or connecting with the inner child.

Our angels know that we appreciate the visual messages that they send us, yet this form of communication is often not enough for us. We yearn to see what our beautiful companions look like! Whenever possible, our angels like to satisfy our curiosity by changing from an invisible force to a visible friend.

How do we know when we actually do see an angel? The angels can appear to us in several ways, depending on our level of clairvoyance.

An angel is often seen as …

- ◆ A sparkle of light.

- ◆ A bright white or colored light around us or in our mind's eye.

- ◆ A colored mist.

As clairvoyance is developed, we may see an angel in a more detailed way, such as …

- ◆ A translucent and colorless form.

- ◆ A shimmering ball of light.

- ◆ A full *apparition* seen with our eyes open.

def•i•ni•tion

An **apparition** is a phenomenon where an ethereal figure appears in an unexpected or extraordinary way.

Aural Communication: Hearing Messages

Most angelic communication is nonverbal, but sometimes we have the ability to hear outside the normal range of sound. Intuitive hearing is called *clairaudience* (clear hearing). This extrasensory gift allows angelic guidance to come to us in all forms of sound, such as words, music, or tones.

If you have clairaudient ability, do not be surprised if you actually start to hear from your angels. You may receive guidance through an internal voice in your head or an external voice in your ear. You may hear your name called out when no one is around. Beautiful celestial music may surround you directly from the angelic choirs.

Most of the time we equate voices in a person's head as a sign of completely losing it, yet this is seldom the case when we are connecting with the angels. Keep your ears open, 'cause the next voice you hear may be the voice of an angel!

Sensory Communication: Feeling Messages

Another form of angelic communication is through *clairsentience* (clear feeling). A clairsentient has the ability to feel and capture information through sensations, often receiving messages through the emotions and senses. This spiritual gift increases our sensitivity and allows us to perceive the subtle vibrations around us.

Divine guidance may come to us through gut feelings, goose bumps, strong emotions, or shifts in air pressure. When we're on the right track, the angels send us feelings of assurance and support. For instance, the atmosphere of the room may change and we may feel surrounded by loving warmth, or we may feel a sudden rush of energy that brings us a sense of deep peace. In times of danger, the angels send us warning energy that is more prickly, such as cold chills or strong waves of apprehension.

When clairsentience is heightened, it's possible for us to feel the touch of an angel. The angels often use the power of touch to comfort us and show us that they love us. Cecily has often felt angel feathers softly caressing her face and a loving hand running through her hair. Some of her students and friends have felt a strong and reassuring hand on their shoulder or felt a sensation that someone was sitting close to them.

Have you ever experienced the sweet scent of flowers carried to you by a warm breeze? You could say that the fragrance is "heavenly." Sometimes our angels use delicious scents such as flowers or vanilla as a calling card to let us know they are nearby. A clairsentient is often able to use their spiritual sense of smell to pick up on these otherworldly scents.

Insightful Communication: Messages Through Knowing

Have you ever just known something without really knowing how or why? This inner knowing is called *claircognizance* (clear knowing).

When we access this intuitive gift, it allows the angels to communicate with us by imparting wisdom directly into our energy field. When our claircognizant abilities are strong, we find that thoughts, ideas, and concepts come to us instantaneously. Suddenly we are able to do things that we were never taught. We acquire insights and inspirations that we never knew or thought about before. For instance, you may know instantly about a current event before you see the news reports, or that nagging thought or idea for a new business venture proves to be a great success.

Opening our claircognizance aids us in navigating through day-to-day life. It is when we embrace the profound knowledge given to us by the angels that we gain the clarity to see the bigger picture. With divine wisdom, we are able to better serve ourselves, others, and the world around us.

Enlightenments

Are some people just more naturally intuitive? Yes, just as some people are more athletically or artistically gifted. Author Sonia Choquette says that those with more natural or heightened intuitive ability are likely to have a soul mission of being a spiritual teacher or guide to others.

What's Your Favorite Channel?

With practice, we all have access to the four types of angelic communication. With that being said, it is common for each of us to possess one primary channel and one secondary channel for receiving guidance. Some will know exactly which of their intuitive channels are the strongest, while others will have to uncover their strengths.

Here are some clues:

◆ Are you naturally visually oriented? You will find that clairvoyance is one of your strongest channels.

◆ Are you drawn to music or have musical ability? You will find that clairaudience is one of your strongest channels.

◆ Are you emotionally sensitive or a touchy-feely type? You will find that clairsentience is one of your strongest channels.

◆ Are you more intellectually minded or highly inquisitive? You will find that claircognizance is one of your strongest channels.

Tuning In

There are several spiritual tools that assist us in opening the four channels of intuitive communication. These tools not only help us access those channels that are weaker, but they deeply enhance our natural abilities as well.

Ways to enhance clairvoyance:

◆ Meditating

◆ Doing guided imagery work

◆ Opening the third eye

Angels 101 _____

To immediately see how open your third eye chakra is, ask your angels to show you your current level of clairvoyance. Next, close your eyes and imagine a rose in your mind's eye. Is the rose closed, partially open, or in full bloom? Go with the first image that pops in your mind. Use how open the flower is as a guide to how open your third eye is.

Ways to enhance clairaudience:

◆ Playing or listening to singing bowls (Tibetan and crystal)

◆ Doing vocal toning (discussed in Chapter 5)

◆ Singing and chanting

◆ Opening the throat chakra

Ways to enhance clairsentience:

- ◆ Emotional releasing

- ◆ Breathwork (deep breathing exercises)

- ◆ Practicing yoga

- ◆ Creative self-expression such as painting, theater, and dance

- ◆ Opening the heart chakra

Ways to enhance claircognizance:

- ◆ Creating a work/life balance; respecting downtime

- ◆ Keeping a journal

- ◆ Working with your hands (woodworking, jewelry making, crafts)

- ◆ Opening the crown chakra

Guided Imagery

The practice of *guided imagery* is often used to strengthen clairvoyance, but it can give a workout to any of the intuitive channels. Guided imagery works energetically. Thoughts and ideas are high vibrating forms of energy and are very powerful in impacting our energy system as a whole. Scientific research has also shown that the same parts of the brain become active when people imagine something or actually experience it. In using all your senses—taste, touch, sight, smell, sound, and intuition—the imagery becomes more "real" to your brain and your energetic field.

def•i•ni•tion

Guided imagery is what you see in your mind's eye, but it can also include broader imagery, such as what you hear, feel, smell, and taste in your imagination. This type of visualization is often led by imagery meditations in books, CDs, or by a practitioner.

The following guided imagery meditation is effective in clearing blockages from the chakra system. Cecily calls it Chakra Clearing Guided Imagery:

Lie or sit in a relaxed and comfortable position with your eyes closed. Your spine should be straight and your head in alignment with your body. Take several deep breaths, inhaling through your nose and exhaling through your mouth. With each exhalation, let the worries of your day start to melt away.

After you are relaxed, become aware of your body from head to toe; feel the heaviness of your limbs. Just "be" with your body, as you go deeper and deeper into relaxation.

Now focus on the area at the base of the spine—the area between your legs. This is the root chakra.

1. Imagine a healthy and balanced chakra as a clear crystal orb filled with a bright red light.

2. In your mind, study the appearance of your own chakra, and note its color and vitality. If your chakra is dusty, dirty, shrunken, or torn, envision a small bolt of lightning blasting away the dirt and defects from your chakra.

3. To completely clean your chakra, send in swirling white light to gently scrub away any remaining debris.

4. Once your chakra is clear, the white light will lift away, revealing a shiny and clear orb with a red glowing energy beneath. Imagine surrounding yourself and bathing in the beautiful red energy. Breathe the glowing red light into all of your energetic system.

Now turn your focus to the area of your reproductive organs (2 inches below your belly button). This is the sacral chakra.

1. Imagine a healthy and balanced chakra as a clear crystal orb filled with a bright orange light.

2. In your mind, study the appearance of your own chakra, and note its color and vitality. If your chakra is dusty, dirty, shrunken, or torn, envision a small bolt of lightning blasting away the dirt and defects from your chakra.

3. To completely clean your chakra, send in swirling white light to gently scrub away any remaining debris.

4. Once your chakra is clear, the white light will lift away, revealing a shiny and clear orb with an orange glowing energy beneath. Imagine surrounding yourself and bathing in the beautiful orange energy. Breathe the glowing orange light into all of your energetic system.

Next, focus on the middle of the abdomen (2 inches above your belly button). This is the solar plexus chakra.

1. Imagine a healthy and balanced chakra as a clear crystal orb filled with a bright yellow light.

2. In your mind, study the appearance of your own chakra, and note its color and vitality. If your chakra is dusty, dirty, shrunken, or torn, envision a small bolt of lightning blasting away the dirt and defects from your chakra.

3. To completely clean your chakra, send in swirling white light to gently scrub away any remaining debris.

4. Once your chakra is clear, the white light will lift away, revealing a shiny and clear orb with a yellow glowing energy beneath. Imagine surrounding yourself and bathing in the beautiful yellow energy. Breathe the glowing yellow light into all of your energetic system.

Now turn your attention to the middle of your chest, to the heart chakra.

1. Imagine a healthy and balanced chakra as a clear crystal orb filled with a bright green light.

2. In your mind, study the appearance of your own chakra, and note its color and vitality. If your chakra is dusty, dirty, shrunken, or torn, envision a small bolt of lightning blasting away the dirt and defects from your chakra.

3. To completely clean your chakra, send in swirling white light to gently scrub away any remaining debris.

4. Once your chakra is clear, the white light will lift away, revealing a shiny and clear orb with a green glowing energy beneath. Imagine surrounding yourself and bathing in the beautiful green energy. Breathe the glowing green light into all of your energetic system.

Now focus on the middle of the throat. This is the throat chakra.

1. Imagine a healthy and balanced chakra as a clear crystal orb filled with a light blue glow.

2. In your mind, study the appearance of your own chakra, and note its color and vitality. If your chakra is dusty, dirty, shrunken, or torn, envision a small bolt of lightning blasting away the dirt and defects from your chakra.

3. To completely clean your chakra, send in swirling white light to gently scrub away any remaining debris.

4. Once your chakra is clear, the white light will lift away, revealing a shiny and clear orb with a light blue glowing energy beneath. Imagine surrounding yourself and bathing in the beautiful light blue energy. Breathe the glowing light blue energy into all of your energetic system.

Next, focus on the middle of your forehead. This chakra is the third eye chakra.

1. Imagine a healthy and balanced chakra as a clear crystal orb filled with a deep blue glow.

2. In your mind, study the appearance of your own chakra, and note its color and vitality. If your chakra is dusty, dirty, shrunken, or torn, envision a small bolt of lightning blasting away the dirt and defects from your chakra.

3. To completely clean your chakra, send in swirling white light to gently scrub away any remaining debris.

4. Once your chakra is clear, the white light will lift away, revealing a shiny and clear orb with a deep blue glowing energy beneath. Imagine surrounding yourself and bathing in the beautiful deep blue light. Breathe the glowing deep blue energy into all of your energetic system.

Now focus your attention to the top of your head. This is the crown chakra.

1. Imagine a healthy and balanced chakra as a clear crystal orb filled with a purple glow.

2. In your mind, study the appearance of your own chakra, and note its color and vitality. If your chakra is dusty, dirty, shrunken, or torn, envision a small bolt of lightning blasting away the dirt and defects from your chakra.

3. To completely clean your chakra, send in swirling white light to gently scrub away any remaining debris.

4. Once your chakra is clear, the white light will lift away, revealing a shiny and clear orb with a purple glowing energy beneath. Imagine surrounding yourself and bathing in the beautiful purple light. Breathe the glowing purple energy into all of your energetic system.

Three Secrets for Enhancing Your Sixth Sense

Awareness, flexibility, and grounding are the three fundamental ways to enhance your intuitive abilities. Angelic guidance can be subtle, so being keenly aware of what is happening around us is essential when communicating with the angels. We live in a world where we are constantly being bombarded by stimuli, and it is common to tune out when we feel we might get overwhelmed. Being in the present is the easiest way to snap back into a healthy state of awareness. Spending time in nature, meditating, and working on creative projects are all ways that bring us into the now or present moment.

Try this awareness exercise:

1. Working with a partner, set up two chairs that face each other.

2. Each person will look at the other for about three minutes, making note of the details of the other person's hair, clothes, jewelry, etc.

3. Next, one person will close their eyes while the other picks two or three things to alter about their appearance (for instance, moving a sock down or taking an earring off).

4. When the person is finished changing their appearance, the other person will open their eyes and try to guess what has been changed.

5. Alternate and repeat the exercise.

When we are working with our sixth sense, it's important to be flexible. Being too controlling can take us out of our intuition. We may not always see, hear, or feel things in a set way, so we must be prepared for the unexpected. When we are flexible and receptive, we are announcing to the Universe that we want to learn new information and try new paths. Coming from a more childlike place helps us loosen up and find joy in new surprises.

To successfully use our intuitive ability, we must learn the practice of grounding. Contrary to some beliefs, intuition does not call for us to be flighty or illogical; in fact, just the opposite is true. In a grounded state we are centered, stable, and balanced. Additionally, when we learn to ground ourselves, we are better able to focus and be in control of our energy. When we are crabby, spacey, flaky, overemotional, or scattered, you can be sure we are in need of grounding. An ungrounded person is often too distracted to pick up on the intuitive signals that he or she is receiving.

There are two powerful ways to get grounded. One way to feel grounded instantly is to hold a large, smooth rock in both hands. Another way is to do a tree meditation. First, stand up straight and tall. Make believe that you are a tree and visualize that your branches extend way up into the sky as high as you can imagine. Next, imagine that your roots are buried deep, deep within the core of the earth. You are now grounded and energetically connected to the earth and the Universe.

It takes practice to become more aware, flexible, and grounded. Expect that these vital qualities should be integrated and infused into your daily life. A simple way of practicing is to focus on areas that naturally bring you into a spiritual state of balance. Each morning, pick one of the following themes and set a goal to make that particular quality a priority throughout your day.

- **Gratitude**—What are you grateful for? Start a gratitude journal.

- **Inspiration**—Who or what are you inspired by? Make a list.

- **Pampering**—What nice things can you do for yourself? Get a massage.

- **Nature**—Where can you go today and be out in natural beauty? Take a bike ride.

- **Play**—How can you have fun? Start a creative project.

- **Retreat**—Where can you go to be alone and rejuvenate? Relax in your backyard.

- **Generosity**—Who can you remember today? Do something special for others and let them know how much they mean to you.

Enlightenments

There is a phenomenon in meditation called the Blue Pearl. This experience of seeing a fascinatingly beautiful, bright blue light while meditating has been known as a sign of enlightenment. Swami Muktananda is a guru who has written of the Blue Pearl and who founded the Siddha Yoga tradition. Muktananda said that seeing it in meditation is like seeing one's soul.

Writing to Your Angels

One of the easiest ways to communicate with your angels is by writing to them. Automatic dictation is the process of recording information that is given to us through our thoughts. You simply say, think, or write a question to the angels and then wait for the response. There is no need to wait for the answer and then write it down; the answer will flow as you are writing. Messages often come quickly and effortlessly; just start with the first word and keep going. The secret is to just receive the information that comes without stopping to analyze it.

When writing to the angels, an old-fashioned pen and paper will do, or you can type on your computer. You are always fully conscious during this process, so there is no danger of giving up control to something outside yourself. Go ahead and ask anything; your angels will respond to any question in the highest and most loving way.

Finding Out the Names of Your Guardian Angels

First relax and clear your mind, then just ask your angels to give you their names. The first name that pops into your head is the name of your most vocal angel. Write it down. Because most of us will have more than one guardian angel, listen for another name to pop into your head. Write the second name down. Wait and listen to hear if any other names come to you. If you receive another name, be sure to put it on your list. Do not be surprised if the names don't sound "angelic" to you. Some angels have distinctly angelic-type names such as Ariel or Celestine, while others have ordinary names such as Bill or Emily.

Angel Art

Do you like to draw? If you do, you might try receiving messages from your angels using a sketchpad and colored pencils.

Spiritual teacher Tina Michelle gets many of her messages through a process called *angel art*. Years ago, Tina was told by the angels to "pick up a pen and draw us." When she is doing an angel reading for a client, she focuses on that person and the angels clairvoyantly morph into various shapes and colors. Tina has worked with the angels over time to develop a language of the shapes and colors given to her. Each hue, shade, and tone carries a different meaning. Often she is shown, told, or guided to draw energy blocks in the person's energetic system. Tina depends on the intuitive channels of clairvoyance, clairaudience, *intuitive empathy*, and clairsentience to receive angel art.

def•i•ni•tion

Intuitive empathy is a heightened form of clairsentience that tunes into other people's emotions, energies, and illnesses.

She has found that what the angels of her clients share with her is truly powerful. The angelic messages found in each drawing are very detailed and often include relevant information related to current life situations.

The angels point out the troubles and circumstances of the person and may explain why particular patterns or events are happening.

Although a more advanced angelic communication technique, those that have an affinity for drawing or painting may find angel art a particularly beneficial and enjoyable way to receive messages.

The Angels in Disguise

The angels have been known to take on a physical body to give us messages or protection during troubled times. Two of Cecily's teachers, Sonia Choquette and Tina Michelle, have each written about a personal experience with a wise and loving human being who profoundly helped them and then just disappeared without a trace. Sonia was having an especially hard time in her life when an angel came to her disguised as a sales clerk in Hawaii and said just the right words to give her the insight she needed. Tina Michelle's face-to-face with an angel happened one night when she was contemplating taking her own life. An angel disguised as a 30-year-old man appeared out of nowhere and helped her regain her sense of purpose. To be of the greatest service to us, the angels will come to our aid in the way we most need it. You never know when you might run into an angel!

Angel Signs

Sometimes the angels communicate with us by sending us signs that anyone can see or hear. One of the most commonly known signs is for the angels to leave a calling card of a feather. Often these feathers are white; however, the angels will use whatever is available to them. The feathers left by the angels may be small fluffy feathers all the way up to large swan feathers and can appear in the most unlikely places. Many of Cecily's students have asked the angels to send them proof that the angels are with them and received feathers as a sign.

You can ask your angels for a sign as proof that you are connecting with them. Let's look at some other common signs.

Clouds

You may see the angels in cloud formations or notice clouds that resemble feathers.

Coins

You may find coins as you walk down the street. The angels leave coins to remind us of our abundance.

Media Messages

If you have asked for angelic help, you may hear the word "angel" mentioned in a song on the radio or on television. When Cecily first asked for a sign from her angels, she woke up to the song "Angel in the Morning" the very next day. Sometimes it is hearing the right words at the right time that serve as a sign from your angels. You may turn on the radio or television and hear the answers that you need to solve a problem, or you may drive by a billboard that has the right slogan or words to bring comfort to you.

License Plates

Much like messages on a billboard, license plates can often have messages from the angels for us. You may find yourself driving behind someone with an inspirational vanity plate that lifts your spirits, or the car in front of you has a plate with the name of a loved one on it.

Small Animals

Repetitive visits by small animals can be a sign from the angels. You may find that the same bird flies to your window for several days in a row or butterflies encircle you when you leave your house. Cecily had a squirrel friend that would often come and sit at her bedroom window and look at her. One day this squirrel was so helpful that she had no doubt that the squirrel was there on behalf of her angels. The evening before an important event, Cecily set her alarm for 6:30 A.M. to make sure she would arrive on time. The next morning as she was sleeping she heard a rapping on her window. She woke up startled to find her visiting squirrel tapping at her window and looking at her. He tapped and tapped until she looked at her clock and realized that it was 6:32 A.M. and that her alarm had neglected to go off. Cecily now says that this was her favorite wake-up call!

Number Sequences

The angels love to use numbers to send us messages. When you start asking for signs, don't be surprised if you start seeing repeating number sequences all around you. Number sequences can be found on digital display clocks, license plates, and even at the checkout counter. You will find that each group of repeating numbers has an angelic message associated with it. 11:11 is a common number sequence; it means you are going through a time of spiritual transformation and spiritual awareness. When you see other repetitive numbers such as 444 or 555, ask the angels what message they are trying to convey to you.

> **Angels 101**
>
> First thing in the morning or before you go to bed are excellent times to communicate with your angels. You are less likely to be distracted and more likely to be in a receptive and relaxed state.

Blocks to Angelic Guidance

Occasionally we are not able to receive clear messages from our angels. Never take this as a sign that the angels do not want to communicate. In most cases, we are blocking the guidance on our end either with our habits or beliefs. Here are some common blocks to angelic guidance.

Too Busy, Tired, or Distracted to Connect

To effectively connect with our angels, we must be still and focused. When we are in a rush, multitasking, or overly tired, we are not in the correct space to receive and comprehend the messages our angels are sending us. Heightened drama in our lives also keeps us out of the intuitive loop. Being caught up in our own drama or the drama of loved ones zaps our energy and hijacks our attention away from more important things. Guided imagery, meditation, and deep breathing help bring us into a receptive state.

Difficulty Understanding Your Angels

Sometimes we need to let the angels know we are having difficulty getting a clear message from them. You can ask your angels for more clarity in each of the four channels of intuitive communication. When you are having trouble understanding the meaning of visual images, ask the angels to clarify the message they are sending you. Ask the meaning of the symbols you are receiving. If you are having trouble hearing what the angels are saying, request that they speak up. You may suddenly know something but not understand the context. Ask your angels to give you the details. A strong emotion may hit you out of nowhere, or you may suddenly find yourself with goosebumps. Ask the angels what your feelings mean.

Feeling Silly or Gullible

What will other people think? This may be the question going through your head when you first start connecting with the angels. You might find yourself wondering if your spouse, partner, friends, or family will think you are strange or delusional when they find out the angels are sending you messages. Some may and some may not, but it is a risk worth taking. The benefits of having the angels in your everyday life far outweigh the potential judgment of others.

Rest assured that using your intuition and communicating with your spiritual helpers is not a fringe phenomenon only for weirdos. Spirituality and spiritual practices have gone mainstream! In 2006, spiritual books had the strongest growth segment in the publishing world with sales topping 263 million. If you still have any doubt, take a look at what Oprah, Ellen DeGeneres, and other media personalities are often buzzing about—personal growth and spirituality.

"Am I making this up?" "What if it's just me?" Sometimes we think we are being gullible if we accept the first message that comes to us. It may come too easily, or the voice in our head sounds similar to our own. Yet when we ask for assistance, most messages that we are hearing, seeing, and feeling are directly from our angels. With time, trust, and practice, we will have a better understanding of which messages are angelic and which are not.

Too Painful to See the Truth

When we've been hiding a part of ourselves or our past, the angels may represent a solid dose of reality. Our angels never judge us, but they know everything about us. With love they tell us the truth in every situation. If we have covered our pain deeply, we may be in denial to this truth when we receive an angelic message. This may cause us to block the message completely, or we may deny that the message is accurate. When you are having difficulty perceiving the truth, ask the angels to help you recover and acknowledge what has been hidden away.

Expecting It to Be Scary

Our clairvoyance can get blocked if we are afraid of what we might see. With the popularity of horror films, it's not surprising that some of us may be hesitant to see the unknown. A deep-seated fear of seeing ghostly or frightening images may shut off our third eye. Another block to seeing beyond the veil is our angels themselves; they will never show themselves to us until we are ready. Ask the angels to assist you in releasing your fears and apprehension. Trust that seeing an angel is a loving, comforting, and beautiful experience.

Expecting Bells and Whistles

It is human nature to want the biggest and the best of everything. This includes intuitive experiences. When we first start communicating with our angels, some of us block our extra sensory channels by having unrealistic expectations. We can become so frustrated that we are not having the exact experience we want, that we end up minimizing or disqualifying any communication that is being sent to us.

For instance, during the years Cecily has found that some of her students are initially so focused on seeing an angel that they miss the feeling type messages and synchronicities that are all around them.

Remember, angelic communication is often subtle. It is best not to have preconceived notions of how your angels will begin communicating with you.

If you want to develop or strengthen one of your intuitive channels in particular, it will take practice. An athlete would not expect to become a champion without practice, and the same holds true for those of us opening our intuitive abilities.

Angels 101

When you are having trouble connecting with your angels, create an imaginary meet-up place and invite your heavenly companions to join you. In a relaxed state, visualize a beautiful and comforting location to interact with your angels. You might select a lush forest or a serene seashore. Journey to whatever type of environment brings you the most joy and relaxation. With all your senses, notice what is around you. What do you feel, see, hear, and smell? The angels will present themselves to you in a way that you can most easily comprehend. You can meet up with your angels in your special spot anytime you wish.

Trying Too Hard

Receiving angelic communication is a flowing process; it is a process of heart over head. When we overthink things or concentrate too hard on communicating with our angels, we block the flow. We often spend so much time up in our heads that it can be difficult to get our minds out of the equation, yet this is exactly what we need to do.

Angelic communication cannot be forced and is not an intellectual practice. So, it is important to let the information just come to us without analyzing each detail. A great way to quiet the mind and let go is to simply enjoy the experience as a child might, without lots of internal dialogue or a need for all the answers.

The Least You Need to Know

◆ We all have intuitive ability and receive angelic guidance through intuitive communication channels.

◆ Angelic communication is often subtle; it's important to learn the language of the angels so you don't miss the signs.

◆ One of the best ways to connect with the angels is through writing.

◆ The angels like to leave us signs as proof that they are with us.

◆ The angels always try to communicate with us, but sometimes our own beliefs and habits get in the way.

Chapter 8

Recognizing Angelic Guidance

In This Chapter

- ◆ Differentiating between authentic and false guidance
- ◆ Messages we often receive from the angels
- ◆ Common signs of false guidance
- ◆ Enhancing our natural gift of discernment

When we first start connecting with the angels, it is common to doubt the guidance that we're receiving as "real" guidance. Don't worry—every good angel communicator started out in the same boat with feelings of doubt and loads of questions. This is a built-in precaution we all have and it actually works in our favor.

The simple fact is that all guidance is not created equally. Although we would like to believe that we are only receiving messages direct from the angels, this is not always the case when communication blocks or low vibrational frequencies keep us from tapping into the angelic energy we seek.

Luckily, there are several rules of thumb that help us easily discern when we are tuned into the angels and when we are not. It just takes a sincere desire to recognize angelic guidance—and a bit of trial and error—to get started.

The Real Deal: Recognizing Authentic Angelic Messages

The angels are sources of divine guidance, clarity, and direction with our highest good and purpose as their main concern. An important angel truth is that their messages always reflect these loving principles in a calm, caring, and patient way. Even during impending danger, angelic communication is consistently supportive and encouraging, not frantic or fearful.

Pay Attention to Language

You will find that the angels do not speak in the same ways that humans do. One of the easiest ways to know if you are in communication with your angels is by observing how they address themselves and you. Because the angels have no ego, they tend to work in groups and call themselves "we" in the plural form. Even if you hope to connect with only one angel, you will always hear "we" instead of "I."

Another telling angel practice is the way they address us in regular angelic conversation. Their tone is formal yet affectionate. The angels do not use casual speech or slang, so don't expect to be called "dude" or "girlfriend." They actually prefer more loving and archaic type nicknames such as "dear one," "beloved," or "dearest."

Angels 101

If the guidance starts with "I," it is most likely from your own ego—for example, "I am on the right track with my career."

The positive and empowering messages of the angels are focused and to the point and sometimes particular words are given to us three times for emphasis such as "Yes, yes, yes." When we write to the angels (see Chapter 7), they tend to be more verbose. On many occasions, Cecily has found that the angels communicate using insightful and poetic type verses during her automatic dictation sessions.

Our angels love to give us suggestions to make our lives better, but they never make demands or tell us what to do. Suggestions are patiently and consistently repeated day after day, until we finally decide to follow them or let them go.

Angel Radar

You will know right away if you are tuned into the angelic realm by using your extrasensory feelings as angel radar. First of all, the angels just feel different than we do. Their guidance may come through our own senses, but it is different enough that we will often find ourselves questioning it. Angelic energy naturally "feels" loving and soothing. In fact, it is common to find that a palpable comforting vibration accompanies each angel message.

Angelic guidance is never nondescript or uninspiring. In fact, a good dose of light energy can leave you feeling safe and calm or revitalized and excited. Often these positive feelings are the after effect of knowing deep down that the guidance is not only true but very meaningful.

Here are some examples of feeling true guidance:

- What you feel in your gut matches the guidance given to you.
- Worrying has been replaced by a sense of peace.
- You have an "aha" moment.
- You have feelings of positive expectancy.

Next steps are clear. You no longer need to flip flop or be indecisive in your area of concern.

Angels 101

Strongly vivid dreams that are easy to recall may in fact contain messages from your angels. In contrast, ordinary, easily forgettable, or confusing dreams have not been touched by your heavenly helpers.

Ask for Signs

The angels are always more than willing to help us discern divine guidance from false guidance. One of Cecily's favorite ways to get confirmation from her angels is by asking them to give her a sign that she is on the right track. She never specifies what type of sign she wants to receive—she leaves that up to her heavenly helpers.

For instance, Cecily was wondering if she would be able to start a family soon. She asked her angels for a sign. Within minutes, she felt a warm knowing wash over her that made her giddy with excitement. Not wanting to chalk it up to wishful thinking, she asked for her angels to give her a back-up sign. A short time later, Cecily walked outside and found that the only other person on her normally busy street was a pregnant woman walking toward her!

Common Angel Messages

Here are common messages we receive from our angels. Notice that all of them are positive:

- ◆ "Patience, patience, patience. It is not yet time, dear one. Divine timing is coming soon."

- ◆ "Dear one, rest now, there is no need to fret. You will soon see that things will work themselves out. Release and do not try to control the outcome."

- ◆ "Dearest, we ask you to take a step back from the situation at hand and observe it from a higher place. All is not what it seems to be. We caution you as you move forward. Watch for the truth to be revealed this week."

- ◆ "Beloved, you are in a place of abundance now. Do not be afraid to move forward and pursue your dreams. Think big and believe in your born right to experience the best in this life. You are a shining star."

- ◆ "Dear one, we are watching over you and sending you much love during these hard times. There is no need to feel alone, for we are always by your side, ready to comfort and support you. All you have to do is ask."

Advice from Above _____

> To properly receive divine guidance, do not edit messages to fit your agenda. The angels may not always tell you what you want to hear, but be sure to listen to the full message because it is always in your best interest.

Warning Signs of False Guidance

What about those moments where you are still unsure about the guidance you are receiving? There are some key warning signs that the messages coming to you are not angelic in nature. False guidance comes in two forms: through our own ego or through less-evolved souls.

The Infamous Ego

Often when we are worried that we are making something up or it is just our imagination, we are referring to our ego taking over and blocking any outside communication. The ego is not a spiritual faculty, but a very human one. The ego is the self, distinct from the world and others at large. In psychoanalysis, the ego is the division of the psyche that is conscious, most immediately controls thought and behavior, and is most in touch with external reality. It is a survival mechanism we have carried with us through life that regularly brings up the same emotional and mental tapes, fears, habits, and baggage every chance it gets.

Our old friend the ego is a master at telling us we are either too good or not good at all. Unlike the angels, it rarely makes us feel comforted, protected, or happy. In fact, it has a knack for leaving us more confused, apprehensive, and anxious than ever before. It could be said that the only time the ego leaves us with fleeting feel-good moments is when it tells us what we want to hear through our own wishful thinking, instead of offering us the true guidance we are seeking.

Enlightenments

In the 1920s, Austrian psychiatrist Sigmund Freud, who founded the psychoanalytic school of psychology, proposed that the psyche could be divided into three parts: ego, superego, and id. The id is the childlike and impulsive portion of the psyche that wants what it wants and disregards all consequences, while the superego serves as the moral compass of the psyche without regard for the bigger picture. The rational ego acts as a mediator seeking balance between the irrational hedonism of the id and the extreme moralism of the superego. A person's thoughts and actions are often most reflected through the ego. When threatened or burdened, the ego may employ defense mechanisms such as denial, repression, fantasy, compensation, and projection. These defense mechanisms are the culprits of guilt, anxiety, and inferiority.

Unreliable Sources

Even with best intentions, once in a while we may turn on the wrong communication channel. Akin to looking for the right frequency on a radio, it is possible for our intuitive antennae to pick up signals from strangers on the other side instead of our angels.

At first thought, we might not be so disappointed. All those that have crossed over have heavenly insight, right? Don't be so sure! Just because someone has passed over to a higher plane does not automatically mean that person is now angelic and wise in nature.

Higher consciousness is available to all; however, because we all have free will, it is not a given that we spiritually evolve when we leave our physical bodies. If a person was mean-spirited, egocentric, or unenlightened on Earth, these qualities may remain in the afterlife. For instance, your grouchy neighbor may have seen the errors of his ways and become patient and kind in death, but he is also just as likely to be the overbearing grump that you remember.

Any guidance we might receive from these lower vibrational souls should be taken with a grain of salt. They may be looking to manipulate someone or in rare cases legitimately try to help. Either way, they do not possess the greater understanding and wisdom of the angels. Our spiritual growth is not important to them, and the guidance they do impart often plays to our ego and not our higher spirit. Less-evolved souls really have no power and can be easily dismissed through angelic protection (see Chapter 9).

Common signs of false guidance include the following:

- Messages that falsely build up the ego—promising fame and fortune or characterizing you as more "special" than others.

- Guidance that makes you feel worried, powerless, scared, or depressed.

- Warnings or predictions of future disasters.

- Messages that are random and ever-changing.

- Messages that leave you with a feeling of negativity.

- Messages that contain gossip or are critical of others.

- Guidance that is confusing or unclear.

- Messages that feel forced and unnatural.

- Guidance that comes as an order and not a request.

Advice from Above

It is not wise to seek angelic messages through Ouija Boards, spirit boards, or angel boards. Although they can seem harmless enough, a majority of psychics and spiritualists (including the famous prophet Edgar Cayce) have found that they tend to open communication channels with less-evolved souls.

The Power of Discernment

The process of honing our powers of discernment takes intuition and trust. Tuning into what we know and feel on an intuitive level actually becomes our greatest guide when receiving messages.

It is important that we listen to those questions or red flags that surface as we assimilate the guidance given to us. Does it feel like inner truth? Is it appropriate for me to follow the guidance? Will this information limit or expand me? Deep down we know what is best for us, so we should only accept guidance that rings true for us in our heart and in our gut. If there is doubt, than there is a good chance that our angels are not part of the equation. Recognizing and using our own internal wisdom leads us to the Highest Guidance.

The Least You Need to Know

◆ All guidance is not created equal. The angels have a distinct way of getting a message across to us.

◆ Feelings can serve as angel radar.

◆ If asked, the angels will gladly give us signs of confirmation after they send us a message.

◆ Our own ego and less-evolved souls are the most common forms of false guidance.

◆ We all know deep down what rings true for us and can detect what guidance is in our best interest.

Part 3

Working with the Angels

Part 3 takes you into the next level of angelic communication. Here you learn about angelic protection and healing, the special bond between the angels and children, and the spiritual connection of soulmates. You also learn about rituals and practices that bring the oh-so-helpful angels and their positive influence into your daily life.

Angelic Protection

In This Chapter

- ◆ Which angels to call on for protection
- ◆ Tips for staying safe in daily life
- ◆ Common energy stealers and the best energy revivers
- ◆ True stories of angelic protection

The angels are our greatest protectors on our earthly journey. Sent by God, they always act in our best interest, keeping us safe from harm when we call on them. In fact, this is what people across the globe often feel is the first line of duty of the angels. Accordingly, they put their faith and trust in God's messengers.

Many people talk of being watched over by their guardian angels. In a 2008 poll by the Baylor University Institute for Studies of Religion, more than half of all Americans believe they have been helped or protected by a guardian angel in the course of their lives. The angels can guard us from everyday accidents, traumas, and negative energy, bringing more safety and peace into our lives.

Asking for protection is never complex, and there is no limit to the number of angels that can be of service to us. However, after we call upon the angels, we may never know how many times these amazing guardians help deliver us from harm each week, each day, or each moment.

Archangel Michael and Protection

Throughout history there have been many stories told of powerful protecting angels, and certainly the most popular of these protectors would be Archangel Michael. Archangel Michael is known as the supreme Archangel of aid and protection. When called, he not only intercedes on our behalf, but also helps eradicate the energy of fear around us and supplies us with courage. When we are feeling afraid or uneasy, Archangel Michael is our most powerful angelic bodyguard.

> **Angels 101**
>
> Spiritual teacher Sonia Choquette asks that the Archangels accompany her throughout the day, one on each side, one in the front, and one behind to watch her back. She always calls in "the archies" (her term of affection for the Archangels) to help her venture forth.

We can call out to Archangel Michael whenever we feel a situation is too overpowering or difficult to handle on our own. For smaller problems, it is always appropriate to call on our guardian angels or the angels of safety.

Protection in Daily Life

Let's face it, today is a far cry from the *Leave It to Beaver* days of the 1950s and early 1960s. We live in a turbulent and often chaotic time where we must maintain a fine balance of protecting ourselves without being overwhelmed, handicapped, or isolated by fear. The angels can give us the extra protection we need without having to jeopardize our happiness or sanity. Wherever our travels take us, the angels will shelter us from harm.

In daily life, where we are often bombarded with all kinds of energy from the public, we can ask for the same type of angelic protection in a crowded mall or an unsafe neighborhood. At our request, guardian angels, Archangel Michael, or the angels of safety will flock to our side when we are in need of angelic shielding. They will clear the negative energy surrounding us and help us release our fear and anxiety by putting us in a calmer state.

When seeking angelic protection, it's important to pay attention to our own inner feelings and intuition. Many times our angels communicate with us through intuitive signals, and if we listen to these "gut" feelings, we can be led out of unpleasant situations or guided to avoid them altogether.

Protection in the Home

Our home may be our castle, but what a home represents is a more valuable treasure. Our home is our sacred space, the place where we can let our guard down. So it makes sense that the time we spend in our house or apartment should be harmonious, peaceful, and safe. There are simple ways to keep ourselves and our families protected from negative energy and violent people both outside and inside our "castle."

Here are some angelic recommendations for protecting the home:

- ◆ **Spring clean every few months**—When we clean our houses by washing walls, cleaning the carpet, rugs, etc., we are helping clear away negative energy that has built up from our family and those who visit us.

- ◆ **Make noise**—Clapping, toning, ringing a bell, and using a singing bowl all help dispel stuck, heavy, negative energy from the home. Go from room to room and make sure to use these methods in each corner of the room, where trapped energy tends to stagnate.

- ◆ **Post the angels to stand guard**—Before you leave the house or go to sleep at night, call forth angelic energy in each room of your house. Then place large angels to form a protective circle surrounding the house. Put two angels on either side of the front door and then an angel in each direction: east, west, south, and north.

- ◆ **Share happy memories**—Photos hold energy. Place happy photos of friends and loved ones around the house for a positive energy lift.

- ◆ **Mist the rooms**—Angelic misting sprays purify your aura and environment. They are usually an infusion of plant and gemstone essences charged with angelic energy. Spray in each room as needed. Use for stuck energy, after negative guests leave, or following an argument. You can purchase misting sprays at fragrance companies such as Aura Cacia or Sanctuary, or make your own angelic misting spray (see the sidebar on the following page).

- ◆ **Use holy smoke**—Burning dried sage plant is an ancient technique for dispelling unwanted energies in the home. Use sage in each room of the house for best results. This is a powerful ritual to use when first moving into a new home; it removes the energies of past homeowners or tenants.

  The sage plant is a shrubby perennial plant in the mint family. Many Native Americans throughout history have used sage for medicinal purposes, as well as religious ceremonies. This highly aromatic plant has been used to cleanse the body, an object, or a given area of negative influences. The burning of sage in religious ceremonies is used to drive out negative thoughts and feelings, and to keep negative entities away.

- ◆ **Set out angelic decorations**—Place angelic pictures and statues around your home for added protection.

Protection in the Car

When we think of all the potential dangers on the road, it's a wonder that the majority of us get where we are going each day so effortlessly and in one piece. Someone or something must be looking out for us, right? Absolutely! Our guardian angels keep us from leaving the earth before our time and if we want more protection while traveling, we just need to ask for it.

Angels 101

To make your own misting spray, choose essential oils such as white sage, lavender, lemon, sandalwood, peppermint, and rose. Look for cold pressed oils.

You'll need the following:

◆ 1 small gemstone of your choice

◆ 30 drops essential oil (such as lavender)

◆ 30 drops essential oil (such as sandalwood)

◆ 1 TB. vodka

◆ ½ cup distilled water

Leave the gemstone in the sun or on a windowsill to charge the crystalline qualities with energy. Mix the essential oils with the vodka. Mix the alcohol-and-essential oil blend with the distilled water in a glass jar with a tight-fitting lid and put the gemstone at the bottom of the jar. Shake every day for a week to help the fragrances mellow and blend. After one week, pour the mixture and gemstone into a 4-ounce bottle with a fine mist spray nozzle.

When Cecily gets into her car, she always calls on Archangel Michael for protection. She then quickly visualizes several angels forming a protective ring around the car. Some of her clients have felt more protected visualizing an angel riding in the passenger seat or the back seat.

Protection in a Plane

For some people, flying can be frightening, for as passengers we must put our lives in the hands of the pilots, mechanics, and the air traffic controllers. The angels reminded Cecily that we must all remember to put our lives in God's hands, too. As God's messengers and as our protectors, the angels can be a reassuring and constant part of our plane travel. Cecily has offered this highly effective angelic protection tip to students and friends. At take-off, call on the angels to join you on your journey. Then imagine a large white angel wing attached to each wing of the plane flapping powerfully to help the plane lift off safely. Whenever you feel nervous throughout the flight, find comfort in the angels being by your side and visualize the strong angel wings protecting the plane and bringing you safely to your destination.

Protecting Yourself

Those with the intuitive gifts of clairsentience or empathy (see Chapter 7) are especially vulnerable to the energies that they come into contact with. An empath or clairsentient is someone who has heightened sensitivity to other people's emotions and sensations of energy, in general. Similar to a sponge, these individuals can soak up so much emotional and energetic information that they become overwhelmed or confused, often taking on outside energy as their own. Those that work with the public or have regular contact with people are particularly susceptible to becoming drained by negative emotional energy.

Be alert. There are three common ways that our energy can be stolen or contaminated:

♦ **Psychic attack**—Someone consciously or unconsciously sends you negative energy. This person may resent you or be jealous of you.

♦ **Psychic vampirism**—A person may be needy, sick, or dysfunctional and in need of a boost. Acting as a human sieve, this individual will unwittingly tap into your energy source, leading to a major drain on your vitality. We have all experienced people who leave us feeling exhausted after only minutes in their presence.

♦ **Psychic debris**—Someone else's negative energy attaches to you and adversely affects how you feel. Similar to a free-floating virus, negative energy can spread from person to person.

Enlightenments

Although it may seem that being an empath or clairsentient creates a rather high-maintenance lifestyle, there are plenty of advantages to having these intuitive gifts. Spiritual coach Alora Cheek, an intuitive empath herself, likes to expound on the power and rewards of those with this highly sensitive nature. More so than a clairvoyant or regular "psychic," she and others similar to her can sense energy; move energy; and because of a stellar ability to read people's feelings, facilitate life-altering transformations.

Angelic Shielding

With all the ways our energy can be stolen and the countless ways we are vulnerable to the outside world, what are things we can do to partner with the angels for the best protection? The angels want to empower us by teaching us to set boundaries with others and the world around us. Weak or unhealthy boundaries attract energy imbalances with others, leaving us drained or in a power play. Likewise, weak boundaries are more apt to attract chaos or lower beings that are no longer in a physical body.

How do we draw the boundaries we need? Here are some of the angels' favorite shielding methods:

- **The white light shield**—When in an uncertain situation or around energy drainers, visualize a bright luminescent white light surrounding you. Or you can imagine putting on a cloak of white light. This is the divine light of the Universe.

- **The blue flames shield**—When in a threatening or frightening situation, visualize bright blue flames radiating around you. These flames of protection are a gift directly from Archangel Michael.

- **Block the solar plexus**—Our solar plexus chakra is the seat of our personal power. When we come into contact with an energy zapper, we can maintain our boundaries by covering the solar plexus with a colored light shield. Visualize a violet or pink shield of light covering the third chakra.

- **The spidey web**—Cecily's spiritual teacher, Sonia Choquette, taught her this protection method and it has become one of her favorites. When in an enclosed space, imagine that you are like Spider-Man with the power to cast webs, except you have webs made of protective light. Simply cast your webs of light to each corner of the room and then imagine them sticking to the top of the ceiling. You can build yourself a protective cocoon of light, no matter where you are.

- **Grounding**—One of the best ways to keep boundaries strong and healthy at the beginning of your day is by grounding yourself by connecting with the earth. Simple morning rituals include grounding meditations; standing or sitting near a tree; digging your bare feet into the earth; or holding a large rock or grounding crystal, such as hematite, obsidian, or tourmaline.

♦ **Wear aventurine**—The aventurine crystal is a light green quartz that acts as an energetic shield around the heart to protect us from other people's negativity. It allows us to be open and loving without being vulnerable. Carry the stone in your pocket or wear it as jewelry.

♦ **Aka cords**—Binding energetic cords between ourselves and the people who matter most to us. Aka cords are created through strong feelings toward and consistent thoughts of a particular person. Cutting these cords with others can be a highly effective energy protector. When you feel bombarded by negative energy or are feeling drained, grouchy, or anxious for no reason, remember to cut cords with everyone that has formed an attachment by calling in Archangel Michael. Say, "I ask Archangel Michael to use his powerful sword and cut all aka cords that have formed between myself and others now." Thank Archangel Michael for his help. You can also use this uncording method as a protective measure when working with the public. Call in Archangel Michael to cut cords throughout the work day. (See Chapter 10 for more about aka cords.)

Angels 101

The blue flame is not the only powerful spiritual fire. There is a highly transformative energy known as the violet flame. By calling on the influence of the violet flame, we can facilitate the elimination of our past mistakes energetically. The violet flame has the power to transmute the cause, the effect, and even the memory of misdeeds in our past. The transmutation process means to alter in form, appearance, or nature. The violet flame changes negative energy into positive energy and darkness into light.

Angelic Cleansing

Just as we need to keep our physical bodies healthy and strong to ward off illness, we also need to keep our vibrational level and energetic system strong to deflect negativity, hostility, and fear. There are four easy ways that we can cleanse our auras and energetic fields to increase our protection:

♦ **Energy healing (Reiki)**—Regular energy healings can remove blockages, clear out negativity, and repair tears in the energy field. They keep our chakras open and spinning and help raise our vibration. (See Chapter 5 for more on Reiki.)

♦ **Spending time in nature**—The ancient Hawaiians knew that the natural world contained plenty of life force energy or mana. We can partake of this healing energy that is all around us and raise our vibration. Mountains, bodies of water (oceans, lakes, seas), and forests hold the most mana. Go outside and tap into the good vibrations.

♦ **Epsom salt and sea salt baths**—Taking a relaxing warm bath with Epsom salt or sea salt is incredibly cleansing to our energetic field. The salts stimulate the flow of energy and help break up and release toxins and negative soot and sludge that are sticking to the aura. Water is also known for its amazing purifying and rejuvenating properties.

♦ **Essential oils**—Plant oils are nature's perfect protectors. They can instantly ground us when we mix them with our energy field and their high vibration can help raise our own. Pass them through your aura by putting a small amount of the fragrance blend in your hand, rubbing your hands together, and then sweeping them up and down your body, about an inch away from your skin. Try eucalyptus, juniper, or frankincense. Aura Soma products work great, too.

Where Were the Angels?

Will the angels be able to stop bad things from happening to us 100 percent of the time when we request their aid or protection? The simple answer is no. If we experience hardships or accidents, this does not mean the angels failed to do their job or were not listening to our prayers. The angels were most certainly there by our side, but they will not save us if an important lesson is involved.

We as humans always associate a happy ending with the best outcome, yet sometimes it is important for us to grow as a soul through some painful lessons. Before our souls entered into the physical world, we requested to learn lessons and do work here on Earth. The ways the lessons are learned are part of our own personal plan to do the greatest good on Earth. On occasion we are conscious of the plan, but often we are not. This tendency for unawareness leads us to experience pain, sadness, and anger when we feel there are injustices in our own lives or the lives of those around us. In contrast, the angels always see God's plan unfolding for the eventual greater good of all involved and have a higher understanding of each situation we experience.

Advice from Above

There is no need to continually or obsessively ask for help or protection from the angels throughout the day. A simple "help, angels" is enough to get their attention and ongoing care.

It is really our job to call on their help and trust that the angels will do that which is God's will. Luckily, 9 times out of 10 it is for our highest good to be protected, guided, and comforted by the angels during challenging or painful times.

Here are a couple of true stories of how the angels helped and served those in need.

Angel of Protection

During my father's battle with emphysema, there was a time two years prior to his passing over that he had a severe attack and lay in the hospital on life support. He was not conscious as family members sat in the waiting room in the small-town hospital of Franklin, North Carolina, and prayed for his recovery. We were not ready to let him go just yet and we then knew that he was not ready to go either.

As I prayed and meditated in the waiting room, I could clearly see as I looked (during meditation, but not physically in the room) at him from the foot of his hospital bed a very, very tall angel to his right. The angel was definitely male, about 10 feet tall and had a golden rope tied at the waist of his long white robes. I do not recall the face, nor do I recall seeing wings, but I told his wife that he would be fine. This angel, I told her, was clearly there to protect him and bring him back.

Indeed my father survived that episode and one night he told his wife that as he lay on life support he was floating around the hospital and knew who was on duty, what the weather was like, and many other things. The clock, however, was spinning wildly he remembered. He also recalled an angel standing next to his bed. She immediately said, "You must call your daughter!" He did and I grilled him. Was it a male presence or female? How tall? What was the angel wearing? Where in the room was the angel? His answers came without hesitation. "A male angel, wearing a white robe and who was very tall, maybe even 10 feet, was guarding me and standing on my right side. I knew I would be okay," he said.

I had to ask without telling him what I had seen because I wanted confirmation. Indeed it was there! I confirmed what he had seen also.

Two years later, when it was time for my father to pass, I sensed the angels again. However, it was clear that they were there to help him pass over to the light. There were a few of them, maybe three or four, and they meant business. It was time to get the show on the road and they were there to help. I never saw their faces, but I felt their presence clearly as he silently passed from this life to the next at 5:30 A.M. on December 26, 1994.

—Denise Painter, Pennsylvania

Saved by an Angel

I was walking along a path made of large, flat, uneven stepping stones while at the Hilton in Hawaii (I would call them "flagstones," but I believe these were made of crushed, pressed coral). My spouse went ahead while I was talking to a guest and he got very far ahead of me. The premises are comprised of many miles, so I bid the new acquaintance good-bye, and I began to run to find him before it would be too late. It was then that one of my open-toed sandals caught the raised part of one of the flagstones sending me into fast forward, down. Falling I remember thinking, "I am going to break my nose, knees, and likely lose some teeth." I also recall shouting, "Angels!" It all happened so fast, but right before my face hit the flagstone, I felt myself lifted, rolled horizontally to my left side, and seemingly dropped ever-gently from someone's arms. I landed on a small piece of soft dirt and grass.

I have been angel clairvoyant since age 5, so I looked up and saw the two rather large helpmates, Archangel Michael and Archangel Raphael. I was very surprised I was not "out cold," and I got to my feet slowly. Feeling the identifiable sting, I looked down to see that each leg had rather nasty bloody scrapes. No one was in sight to help, so I took a move slowly. My legs worked. I touched my teeth and they were all firm. So I took a look in a little mirror, and amazingly, there was not a mark on my face. As I walked one pace at a time to get to first-aid for the injuries I did have, I could not help repeating, "Thank you, Angels!"

—Nancine Meyer, Arizona

The Least You Need to Know

♦ The angels are our greatest protectors on Earth.

♦ Archangel Michael is our most powerful angelic bodyguard.

♦ Energetic shielding and cleansing of our energy field are the most common ways we receive protection.

♦ Our friends, relatives, and the public at large often unwittingly drain energy from us on a regular basis.

♦ The angels want to empower us to set boundaries with others and to keep our energy fields strong and vibrant.

Healing with the Angels

In This Chapter

- ◆ How the angels heal
- ◆ Top blocks to divine healing
- ◆ Determining the best ways to ask for healing
- ◆ Uncording to release unwanted influences
- ◆ Angelic healing for relationships, illnesses, addictions, emotions, and others
- ◆ Healing the world

An important mission of the angels is healing. Service is their first concern, so it is their duty and pleasure to do such important work for humanity. Healing with the angels is often a profound and life-changing experience, as they restore health, balance, and wholeness to our lives. Because the angels always act on God's will, angelic healing is actually God's healing. The angels tap directly into the healing power of God as they perform wondrous healing miracles.

Don't think this means the angels sit back and let God do all the work. There are no slackers here. The angels act as important conduits and messengers of healing energy. Plus, because they can see the big picture these heavenly beings always take their job seriously. When they offer to be in service to each of us, the angels understand that they are healing the world one person at a time.

The Power of Angelic Healing

Cecily once visited a Spiritualist Church to listen to the minister talk about spiritual healing. The elderly female minister had learned about the power of spiritual and angelic healing through her own battle with several illnesses. She had been cured of cancer twice, lived through a deadly brain tumor, plus she overcame a multitude of other serious illnesses since she was a young woman. Cecily was shocked. How could this woman still be alive and in good health? It sounded as if she had nine lives. The minister explained that it was through her faith and will to live, prayer, and healing from angelic energy that she was still alive and kicking. The minister also saw miraculous healings among her congregation during 35 years' time. From the healing of toothaches to the treatment of drug abuse, she saw it all.

Enlightenments

The Spiritualist Church arose from the Spiritualist movement which began in the 1840s in America. The Spiritualist service is usually conducted by a minister who is also a medium. There is an opening prayer, a sermon, hymns, and contact with the angelic and spirit worlds.

Healing with Universal Energy

While reading the Spiritualist Church story, you may be both amazed and perplexed by an example of someone repeatedly beating the odds. The notion of healing without medicine and science can seem like a pretty abstract concept.

In truth, angelic healing is fairly abstract but no less real or effective than more customary forms of therapy. Instead of medical procedures, prescriptions, and textbook diagnosis, the angels rely on the strength of Universal energy. Often, it takes this higher form of energy to effectively transform any emotions, thoughts, patterns, and programs that underlie our ill health and our dysfunctional relationships.

Love Is the Answer

The healing energy of the angels can come to us in many forms including light, vibration, sound, symbols, divine insights, and colors. It may sound cliché, but the secret to activate these special healing powers is the energy of love. Yes, pure and flowing love. With an infusion of Universal love, balance and healing can begin. Without loving energy, no healing is ever effective. The angels work to open our hearts, so we can accept the healing energy they offer. Our heart connects us directly to God, so their first line of business is to clear our heart chakra of blockages, old beliefs, and negativity.

After our heart energy is strong, the angels then purify, balance, and integrate the chakra centers (see Chapter 5) and align our energetic bodies with higher consciousness. This is very powerful in clearing and healing issues and illnesses on all levels. Some people may actually feel the healing as a subtle caressing vibration or as a wonderful, expanding warmth.

Cecily recommends this heart connect guided imagery for all-purpose healing:

1. Close your eyes and relax, taking several deep breaths.

2. Imagine a deep glowing green orb in front of you. Notice how the orb gently shifts into a beautiful and noble angel. This is Archangel Raphael.

3. Next, watch as a glowing pink orb forms in front of you. The orb moves and spins and you see that a glorious angel has appeared. This is Archangel Chamuel.

4. Notice how your heart center chakra opens to the presence of these two powerful angels. Green and pink lights illuminate you and shine directly into your heart chakra.

5. Feel the love and warmth surrounding you. The angels are healing your heart, replacing fear with Universal love.

What the Angels Require from Us

Angelic healing requires our assistance. It is not enough to just stand by and let the angels work their healing magic. We must be active participants in the process.

Increasing self-awareness is an important factor in healing. The angels need us to recognize our self-defeating behavior and thoughts, so that they can effectively aid us. This is the prework before a big healing can come. Sometimes healing can only be accomplished if we peel away our defenses and negative patterns layer by layer and let our true essence shine through. Most of us forget who we truly are with the strains of daily life, so we must wake up and remember that our essence is pure, loving, and wise—created in God's image.

Oftentimes we define ourselves through the lens of our experiences. We carry with us core beliefs about ourselves and the world around us from childhood. These childhood beliefs and patterns are programmed into us deeply.

If negative patterns are not brought to the surface and identified, over time they can build momentum and lead to problems in every area of our lives. Luckily, negative programs can be replaced with positive ones. We will be looking at the two main beliefs that hold us back from healing.

The Unworthiness Factor

One of the biggest impediments to healing is feeling unworthy. When we feel unworthy of love or goodness, we are essentially telling the Universe that we are unworthy of healing. The Universal energy is love. Each time we do not feel entitled to love, we are cutting off the main ingredient to the healing recipe.

Many times unworthiness is the culprit that created the illness and issues in the first place. When we deny love, we deny ourselves the ability to receive and express what comes from our heart. A blocked heart causes imbalance and eventually sickness in our bodies and relationships. An intervention is needed to find self-love without depending on outside validation.

With the angels' assistance, we can learn to embrace all parts of ourselves, good and bad, and see ourselves as complete and whole—the way that God made us. Life becomes better when we believe we are loveable. For when we are open and warm and caring and send out loving vibrations, the world responds favorably.

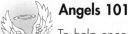

Angels 101

To help encourage self-love and self-esteem, make a list of what you love about yourself. Don't be shy. Think of at least 20 things.

Letting Go of Victimhood

Another trap we might find ourselves in is holding on to the belief that we are victims to the whims of God and those around us. This type of victim mentality can be very crippling because it dictates that we have no control over our lives. When we hold this belief system close to us, we often think illness or trouble is our lot in life or we are being punished by God. The angels know that humanity has no victims, and they wish to help us realize this essential fact.

Even when life seems to be spinning out of control, God is not withholding love or punishing us. Life on Earth is a school where we come to learn lessons. Tests are in the form of difficulties, challenges, and problems. We would not grow mentally, emotionally, physically, or spiritually without these tests. Bad times can be opportunities for us to understand on a much deeper level how much love is available in any situation—good or bad.

Little healing can be accomplished without a clear choice and positive intention from the person that requires healing. Powerlessness does not work. This is why the angels need us to feel empowered by our God-given gift of choice. When not playing the role of the victim, we always have a choice in every situation. A prayer in the spiritual guidebook, *A Course in Miracles*, says that every decision we make is a choice between grievance and miracle.

The Healing Toolkit

There are many different ways to help the angels heal you. Just like carrying around your favorite tools in a toolkit, imagine that each of these methods is available to you at any time for therapeutic repair and service in your daily life. Simply pull these techniques out of your proverbial "toolkit" and use them to bring in the angels for powerful healing.

Say a Little Prayer

The quickest and most effective way to receive angelic healing is through prayer. Prayer is God's hotline. When a prayer is sent to God, the angels are standing by to act as messengers for those in need.

Healing Rainbows

The healing energy of the angels can be seen clairvoyantly as colored light. Using this gift of clairvoyance, colored light can be seen in the mind's eye or with eyes open as an expanding and glowing colored shape representing the healing energy direct from the angels. The angels channel this colored light into our own aura or the auric field of others, and in and around organs in the body that need healing.

These colored-light frequencies carry the therapeutic properties of the represented color. The angels know just what form of color therapy will be the most beneficial for our special needs. For those who want to participate in the process, pick a color. You can request your own healing color infusion.

Each color has different energy and healing frequencies.

Blue promotes:

- Calm and relaxation to counteract chaos or agitation
- Inspiration and the flow of communication
- Solitude and peace
- Sleep

Pink promotes:

- Caring and tenderness
- Love
- Self-worth and self-acceptance
- Forgiveness

Red promotes:

- Increased enthusiasm and interest
- Passion
- Action and confidence to go after your dreams
- Vitality

Orange promotes:

- The ability to adjust to change
- New beginnings
- Increased creativity
- Lightheartedness and humor

Green promotes:

- Balance and healing
- Fertility
- Change and growth
- Freedom to pursue new ideas
- Learning

Purple promotes:

- Heightened imagination
- Meditation and introspection
- Psychic awareness
- Spirituality

Yellow promotes:

◆ Clarity for decision-making and awareness

◆ Sharper memory and concentration skills

◆ Protection from lethargy and depression

◆ Relief from emotional burnout, panic, nervousness, and exhaustion

◆ Self-expression

Gold promotes:

◆ Increased personal power

◆ Good health

◆ Success

Black promotes:

◆ A sense of potential and possibility

◆ Preparedness for the unknown

White promotes:

◆ Kindness

◆ Purification of thoughts or actions

◆ Protection

Enlightenments

Strictly speaking, black and white are not colors. Black is the absence of all color and white is the presence of all colors in the spectrum. When people speak of opposites, it is usually in terms of black and white. Black absorbs all aspects of light. While white reveals, black conceals. White stands for wholeness and completion. In many cultures it represents openness and truth, while black has come to mean what is hidden. It is linked to the unseen or the unknown.

Uncording

Whenever we send out thoughts or feelings to others, we send an energy impulse to them. When these thoughts and feelings become strong and consistent, we form a binding energetic cord between ourselves and the people that matter most to us. In Hawaiian mysticism, these etheric cords are known as *aka cords* and consist of energy patterns that can be visualized as light, elastic cords. Over time, the cords can become stronger and appear as thick as ropes. These cords cannot be seen with the naked eye, but can be seen clairvoyantly and felt through clairsentience.

def•i•ni•tion

Aka cords are strong strings of energy built between us and those we care about. They are only visible to the clairvoyant and felt by the clairsentient.

Although these aka cords occur naturally, they do not serve us. Having heavy ties between ourselves and certain others may not always be in our best interest. Energy flows through the aka cords and as a result we take in other people's feelings, both good and bad. Often these cords act as a drain on our energy.

Cutting aka cords, also known as uncording, is a liberating experience that leaves us free to move forward. Simply ask Archangel Michael to cut these unwanted cords with his sword. Say, "I ask Archangel Michael to use his powerful sword and cut all aka cords that have formed between myself and others now." Thank Archangel Michael for his help. You can perform this ritual anytime you feel you need it. Do not be concerned that you will lose a connection with your loved ones; you will just cease to have an unhealthy energetic bond.

Healing with Archangel Raphael

You can call on Archangel Raphael for help when you are in any kind of pain, whether it is physical, emotional, intellectual, or spiritual. Archangel Raphael supervises healing for humanity. He surrounds and nurtures people with the emerald green light of healing. Except in situations where a person's death or illness is part of their overall divine plan, Archangel Raphael will energetically promote healing. Look for him to inspire you with sudden insights giving you just the right information to help the healing. Archangel Raphael is also a motivator for those in the healing profession. He regularly assists doctors, surgeons, and psychologists in medical intervention.

Healing Relationships

Drama does not make the world go around, it just seems that way sometimes! Everyday relations with our loved ones can sometimes feel like a rollercoaster ride that we just can't get off of.

Relationships can raise us to our highest highs or sink us to our lowest lows. We all have those times where no matter what we do, we are unable to come to a peaceful agreement with another person.

Luckily, the angels are adept catalysts for healing relationships. By asking the angels to aid us, we can ease the drama in our lives and have a deeper and more satisfactory connection with others.

For healing to take place, the angels first need for us to see things from their higher spiritual vantage point, so we don't get bogged down in petty ego conflicts. The angels can easily see the bigger picture and are witness to the self-defeating patterns and behavior that get us into trouble in relationships.

One of the most common reasons for relationship difficulties is our unconscious defense mechanisms. Conflict often stems from how each person feels about his- or herself. For instance, when a person believes they are unlovable they can behave in unlovable ways. As the old saying goes, people need loving the most when they deserve it the least. Illuminating, right?

Yet this is only the half of it. It is not just how we act, but how we react to others. Frequently, these same beliefs about ourselves put us on the defense when someone pushes the right button. If someone makes us feel bad, they have plugged into a negative belief we hold about ourselves.

Other times, our biggest roadblock to healthy relationships can be our own shadow, or the unacceptable part of ourselves that we like to deny. Our suppressed aspects are often the same things we despise in others. When we find ourselves judgmental or intolerant over little things, it is time for us to look a bit deeper and find out what we don't accept in ourselves.

Acknowledging and recognizing our negative patterns and behavior is a great first step toward healing, but it is through love and forgiveness that we actually close the circle. The angelic mantra for relationships is "love more, forgive more." In rising above day-to-day power struggles, the angels encourage us to use the strength of love and forgiveness as the ultimate band-aid. In adopting an attitude of compassion in our relationships, we can clearly see that any negativity is actually a cry for more love.

The presence of love can cut through all the conflict that exists between people. Through prayer, the angels will bring us guidance and courage to forgive and love those that have hurt or wronged us. They can also send us healing light to mend imbalances and bring more harmony into our relationships.

Here is a prayer Cecily recommends for healing relationships:

> Beloved God, please help me infuse my relationships with love, compassion, and understanding to bring about much needed healing. Send me and my loved ones currents of healing love and light to triumph over the fear that has caused us sorrow. Aid us in seeing things from a higher perspective and give us the ability to feel what it is like to be in another's shoes. Most of all, help us find loving forgiveness for any harm that we have caused each other.

Following is a guided imagery for healing relationships:

1. Close your eyes and take several deep breaths. With each breath you take, breathe in healing green light.

2. Imagine yourself in an open field under a blue sky. There is a small hill in front of you. Watch as the person you would like healing with walks over the hill toward you.

3. Ask the Angels of Relationships to surround you and the other person. Watch as they send beams of healing light (notice the color) between your heart and the heart of the person in front of you.

4. Feel the healing warmth run through your body. As you receive the angelic healing, send thoughts of love and forgiveness to the other person.

5. Once the healing is complete, you will notice that the healing light slowly dims and that the angels move away from the circle.

6. Thank the angels and imagine embracing the person in front of you.

Healing Illness

From a small cut to a devastating illness, the angels can be counted on to send us the healing energy of God. Angelic healing is detoxifying, cleansing, and therapeutic. When we are in pain, they comfort and soothe us with their loving presence. If it is God's will, we often find that a miracle can happen. For instance, the doctor diagnoses a man with terminal cancer and during the next checkup he is suddenly cancer-free. The angels have healing powers that know no bounds.

The angels work as wonderful complements to medical science. Not only do they have divine energy at their disposal, but they know the root of each illness. Disease and illness is rarely just physical, as repeat negative thoughts and emotions can cause energetic blockages that grow into illness.

Our heavenly helpers can zoom in on the emotional or psychological cause of our imbalances and aid us in transforming our dark, negative energy to clear, vital energy. We can ask the angels to send healing light vibrations to blockages or areas of discomfort in our bodies.

Here Cecily recommends a prayer for wellness:

> Beloved God, I ask that you infuse my body with health and vitality. Help me to let go of any negative thought patterns, habits, and energetic blocks that have caused an imbalance in my body. Please dissolve my illness (or illnesses) and ease my discomfort. Most of all, aid me in perceiving my body as whole, strong, and healthy.

Following is a guided imagery for healing illness:

1. Close your eyes and take several deep breaths. With each breath you take, breathe in healing green light.

2. Slowly scan your body and organs in your mind's eye and identify the places in your body that need healing.

3. Call upon your guardian angels and the Angels of Physical Healing to surround you.

4. Watch and feel the pulsating currents of green healing energy that they send your body. You may notice a shower of healing energy all over your body or light being directed at one or several parts of your body individually. Wherever the angels send the light is appropriate for your healing. The healing light may pulsate for several minutes.

5. Once you feel the healing subside in your body, watch as the angels send a new powerful stream of expanding green light from you up to the sky. Let it travel up into the Universe as high as you can imagine. Then take the healing light down as far into the center of the earth as possible.

6. Once the healing is complete, you will notice that the green light slowly dims and that the angels start to move away from you.

7. Thank the angels.

> **Advice from Above**
>
> The angels ask that we forget the concept of incurable when we think of our health and well-being. For angelic healing to be effective, we need to believe that we should be healed, deserve to be healed, and can be healed. Feelings of doubt and undeserving can cause a barrier to healing energy.

Healing Addictions

In our society, addictions and compulsions devastate lives every day. Severe addictions are like a ticking time bomb, especially those that can prove to be fatal over time, such as drug and alcohol dependency. Even seemingly innocent addictions can have harmful effects. Too much caffeine can put a strain on our adrenal glands. Too much time spent playing video games can isolate us from others.

Compulsive behaviors are really coping mechanisms for dealing with life. Instead of handling the uncertainty of each day in a constructive and balanced way, those with addictions often use substances or repeated behaviors to gain a false sense of confidence or to numb out so they don't have to feel or truly participate in life.

Most individuals with severe addictions are striving to satiate a need for stability and wholeness they never had in childhood, and are very often looking for ways to escape the painful emotions that are bubbling up inside them from prior abuse or traumatic experiences. Using addictive behaviors as a camouflage technique may work for a short period of time, but ultimately they become a liability. When we become dependent on something outside of ourselves and God to get us through the day, it is time to ask for divine intervention.

The angels very much want to help those who are suffering from addiction. By offering spiritual, physical, emotional, and mental support to those in need, they can serve as powerful aides in the recovery process. More so than any addiction professional or program, the angels know us intimately and can be our biggest champions as we strive to get our lives on track. We can always count on our heavenly helpers to act as an amazing support team to any professional addictions treatment.

Here is an addiction healing prayer Cecily recommends:

> Beloved God, please help me recognize more joy in my life, so that I do not have to seek false and short lived fulfillment through my addiction(s). Aid me in truly feeling my emotions, so I am no longer numb to my worldly experience. Assist me in forgiving abuse that I have suffered in my past. Help me connect with the wise part of myself, that is passionate about my life purpose and gifts I have to share. Most of all, assist me in seeing the greatness of my soul and remind me that I am worthy of true abundance.

Guided imagery for healing addictions:

1. Close your eyes and take several deep breaths. With each breath you take, breathe in healing green light.

2. Imagine yourself in a beautiful and tranquil garden. Flowers of all colors and shapes surround you, beckoning you deeper into the garden. Heavenly floral fragrances drift in the air.

3. As you walk through the garden, you come upon a wooden door. You push on the door and are able to enter into a secret garden.

4. This garden is not like the bigger garden that surrounds it, for it contains only weeds. All the plants and flowers that had once grown there had been long forgotten and were left to wither and die. These weeds represent your addictions and secrets.

5. Call on your angels to help you get rid of these weeds. Watch as your heavenly helpers appear one by one in front of you. Notice how they immediately join in, clearing the garden one weed at a time.

6. As each weed is plucked, it is transformed into a magical colored seed. Only a pile of seeds is left remaining. The angels instruct you to take the seeds and plant them in the rich soil that has been uncovered in this secret garden.

7. With each seed that you plant, a gorgeous flower instantaneously blooms. Soon you find yourself surrounded by a sublime and bountiful garden. All your weeds are gone.

Healing Our Emotions

In the course of a day it is not unusual to go through a full range of emotions. We may start the day happy, but if our day plays out like a bad movie, we could very well end the day in a state of anxiety, anger, or sadness. This is not surprising as our emotions are often the lenses through which we look at the world; when things are going our way, we feel positive emotions, and when things are difficult, we often find negative emotions take over. It's the negative emotions that are the uncomfortable ones, and we often work hard to suppress or deny them. This is where we sometimes get into trouble.

Emotions such as guilt, anger, and depression do not actually go away when we don't express them, but instead become trapped toxins in our energetic fields. This is why it is so important to acknowledge that all emotions are natural, because, after all, emotions are a big part of the human experience.

Even highly evolved spiritual masters have not gotten rid of strong emotions; they have just learned to channel them constructively. The angels want to help us do the same thing. They understand that for us to be healthy and balanced, we need to acknowledge and express deeply trapped emotions from the present and the past. The angels assist us in releasing our stuck emotions through divine insights, nurturing guidance, and healing light energy.

Here is a healing prayer for emotional release that Cecily recommends:

> Beloved God, please help me get in touch with all my emotions, however uncomfortable they may be, so that I can release and transmute them. With your assistance, let me fully be a part of the human experience by embracing all parts of my human self, the good and the bad. Give me compassion and understanding for my shadow side, so I can better shine my light. Most of all, remind me that each part of myself is worthy of love and blessings.

Guided imagery for emotional release:

1. Close your eyes and take three deep breaths. With each breath, feel yourself becoming more and more relaxed.

2. Imagine yourself on a peaceful tropical island. Beautiful flowers and trees surround you as you walk along a winding path.

3. You find yourself in a clearing with a glorious waterfall rushing into a crystal clear pool of water. This is the place that you will meet your angels.

4. One by one, illuminated beings join you. Notice the colors of your angels as they appear. They have come to help you release the emotional blocks that are in your way.

5. Think about each feeling, emotion, and habit you would like to release and hand over to the angels. As each feeling, emotion, and habit comes into your consciousness, imagine it forming into a hard stone.

6. Throw each stone into the crystal pool of water before you. There is no need to hold back; get rid of all those negative blocks in your energy field.

7. When you are finished, watch as your angels collect the stones at the bottom of the pool with a large golden saucer.

8. Thank them as they take flight carrying the saucer of stones far away.

Angels 101

An effective way to find hidden emotions is by noticing them as they come up. Where does the emotion reside in your body? If the emotion were a color, what color would it be?

Healing Others

So what about asking for angelic healing for our loved ones? Many of us want to help others find comfort and peace, and it is certainly a loving act to ask God for angelic assistance. Because each person can choose whether to accept healing from the angels, it is not a violation of free will. Simply say a prayer to God asking for the divine healing of a loved one in need. Let expectations go and put it completely in God's hands. The level of healing is directly affected by the conscious and unconscious will of the recipient.

Some individuals welcome the healing, and others turn it away. "Why would anyone turn healing away?" you may ask. In most cases there is fear associated with the healing. Some do not trust the energetic healing process, while others are being served by the illness and do not want to get better. For example, they may be receiving more attention and love than ever before and they fear it will disappear when they get well.

Freedom, choice, and respect are always given to everyone and the angels will never force healing on an individual, no matter how ill they may be. With that being said, they will never give up on anyone either. Expect that the angels will be on standby to send healing light at just the right time.

Here is a prayer for healing others that Cecily recommends:

> Beloved God, please heal (add name). He/she is in need of your Divine grace and Divine light now.

Following is a guided imagery to send healing to others:

1. Close your eyes and take several deep breaths. With each breath you take, breathe in healing green light.

2. Call on your guardian angels and ask them to connect with the guardian angels of the person in need of healing. Request that the person's guardian angels send healing light to areas (body, mind, emotions) that person most needs it.

3. Thank your guardian angels.

World Healing

Earth and all the people inhabiting it can benefit from the power of angelic healing. When we open our lives to the angelic realm, the idea of "peace on Earth" often becomes an aspiration and not just a thoughtful slogan on a bumper sticker. Prayer can send showers of divine, healing light across the planet. Send healing to all parts of the globe; send it for famines, natural disasters, war, strife, and poverty. Send it to heal rifts between nations and to end corrupt governments. Even send it to peaceful areas to keep them protected. Our prayers have the ability to create miracles.

The most effective prayers are those without judgment and anger. Surround your prayers with love and forgiveness for those across the world. If you are having trouble with forgiveness, then send your prayers in a state of neutrality.

Here is a prayer for world healing that Cecily recommends:

> Beloved God, please send your powerful blessings and healing to the world. Send the people of the world and the environment currents of healing love and light to triumph over the fear and neglect that have swept across our earthly home. Aid those in need of your grace and love now.

Following is a guided imagery for world healing:

1. Close your eyes and take several deep breaths. With each breath you take, breathe in healing green light.

2. Select the part of the globe you would like to heal or simply imagine the whole world in your mind's eye. What color light is surrounding the continent, country, or area you are thinking of? What color light does the world have around it?

3. Call on the Angels of World Healing. Ask them to show you the color of light that will best heal the selected area, region, or whole world itself. Watch as the light around the world or region changes from the first color you saw to the new healing color as the angels start their work.

4. See the angels join a circle around the region or world, creating a greater concentration of light that completely fills up the space with pulsating healing energy. The healing may take several minutes.

5. Once the healing is complete, you will notice that the colored light slowly dims and that the angels start to move away from the chosen area.

6. Thank the angels.

The Least You Need to Know

◆ Angelic healing is actually God's healing. Love is the most powerful source of healing.

◆ Self-defeating behaviors often block us from healing energy.

◆ Each color in the spectrum contains unique and essential healing properties and characteristics.

◆ Uncording is a powerful healing practice that creates healthier bonds between ourselves and our loved ones.

◆ The angels use the high frequencies of colored light to generate transformational healings to our relationships, emotions, and physical health.

◆ Healings can be individual or on a large scale. The potent energy of the angels can assist in healing just one person or healing the whole world.

Chapter 11

The Angels and Children

In This Chapter

- The special connection between kids and the angels
- Children's attunement to the spirit world
- Indigo Children, a new type of child
- How children can use their intuition

Small, innocent, and pure of mind, children have always had a special, intuitive connection to the spirit world—and specifically to the angels.

Here we discuss the ways children and the angels interact, what we can learn from the connection, and most importantly, how we can foster and encourage the relationship.

Why Children Have a Special Relationship with the Angels

Children are beautiful in that they are always fully present—they live in the here and now, giving them a high awareness of their environment.

There is a connection to the Spirit that children naturally have for three reasons:

♦ Closeness to the spirit world

♦ Open-mindedness

♦ Playfulness

Closeness to Spirit

Children were recently born, so they just left the spirit world. To better understand, think about a trip or vacation you just took last year. You can probably describe the locale, the people, the food, and other details. Now try to remember a trip you took a decade ago. There are trace memories, little details that really made an impression on you, but your recollection will probably be foggier than that of the more recent trip. The same idea applies to children and adults. They simply were in the spirit realm more recently than we were and are closer to the pureness and wisdom of the Divine.

> **Advice from Above**
>
> Children may have an easier time opening up to the angels and the spirit world, but we are just as capable as adults. The main thing we can do is learn from the ways of children—to become open-minded, joyous, and loving.

Open-Mindedness

Children are not as assimilated as we are into the rigid belief systems of society. As a child, you see the world through eyes of wonder, because you are not yet jaded by the harshness of the outside world. You have not built up strong fears, beliefs, and worldly experiences that often cause us to shut down our trusting and open nature as we get older. Plus, children are comfortable and adept at using their intuition, often moving on instinct, not logic.

Most modern educational systems put the emphasis on logic and other left-brain exercises such as math and science, while numbing our right-brain traits such as intuition, imagination, and creativity. However, there are some progressive schools and children's programs that cultivate right-brain skills as much as traditional left-brain logic. Research schools and programs in your area; you may be pleasantly surprised at what new, innovative curriculums are available for your child.

Playfulness

The angels know the importance of light-hearted play! Fun, laughter, and joy are ways to express a love of life. As adults, we tend to consider "excessive" playfulness to be immature and undesirable. As children, however, we easily emote these feelings of happiness.

The angels appreciate how children express their positive feelings and always encourage adults to do the same.

Children and Animals

Children are more sensitive and intuitive than adults, so they are more receptive to the spiritual realm. Popular in Native American culture, animals can actually be spirit guides known as power animals. Any animal on Earth can be deemed a power animal, with a basic purpose to share their attributes and energy with humanity. For instance, one might call on an owl for wisdom or a lion for courage. Children naturally connect with animals around them, as if they intuitively understand the connection between animals and Mother Nature, so it is no wonder that animal spirit guides are drawn to them as well.

Children can easily draw special energies from their animal spirit guides to make their lives easier and to feel more protected.

Try this exercise:

1. Ask your child to close his eyes and imagine his favorite animal.

2. Tell him to visualize that animal protecting him wherever he goes.

3. Tell him that the animal is a part of him. The animal will never go away.

Enlightenments _____

We discuss animals here, but it need not be a traditional mammal. It could be a mythological creature such as a dragon or unicorn or even an original, wonderful beast described by your child. The point is to help your child feel safe and connected to its friendly being and the spirit guide it represents.

There are many immediate benefits to children connecting with a power animal. The process can help them with:

♦ Self-esteem

♦ Bullying

♦ The mind-body connection

♦ Separation anxiety

♦ Loneliness

♦ Fear

Indigo Children

Indigo is the color radiating from the third eye, the chakra that represents psychic and intuitive abilities. *Indigo Children* are a group of spiritually enhanced kids in the new millennium that are meant to usher in a new world of hope, faith, and love.

As emotionally sensitive people, many Indigo Children are born with an intuitive gift, such as clairvoyance, or a healing ability. It is common that they speak openly about the angels and other spiritual guides that

they see until discouraged by others. It is so important to protect
and cultivate the natural intuitive
abilities of children, so that they
feel safe using and expressing
their sixth sense. The more they
are encouraged, the better world
they will create in the future.

def•i•ni•tion_____

Indigo Children are a group
of ultra-sensitive and highly
intuitive kids meant to take
humanity to the next level.

Their high sensitivity usually manifests in a certain physical way. For
instance, some Indigo Children cannot handle loud noise or music,
while others are fragile to touch. A common characteristic is adapting
to the mood of other people—crowds or other chaotic groups can make
them feel emotionally vulnerable.

You might say the Indigo Children seem wise beyond their years.
These children naturally have a higher sense of self and a strong self-
worth that foster a sound belief in both themselves and their mission. Nothing gets past these kids—often speaking up for themselves,
expressing themselves freely, and seeing beyond the deceptions and lies
of others are all hallmark traits of the Indigo. As examples of honesty,
they call us to all be more in alignment with our integrity.

Indigo Children naturally have a higher spiritual understanding, so
they can have a difficult time with absolute authority (without choice
or explanation) or simply going with the flow. It's like they intuitively
know that our current way of doing things is outdated—in which case,
what's the point of continuing?

Parents and other authority figures with Indigo Children serve them
best by ...

◆ Respecting their space and viewpoint.

◆ Encouraging them to express themselves both emotionally and
creatively.

◆ Listening to what they have to say.

◆ Challenging them with new and fun ideas.

Enlightenments

Many spiritual practitioners believe that the influx of Indigo Children is the reason for the increase in diagnoses of ADD (attention-deficit disorder) and ADHD (attention-deficit hyperactivity disorder). It's as if some Indigo Children move at a different vibration and have a difficult time adjusting to the speed of our world.

To learn more about Indigo Children, you might want to check out *The Complete Idiot's Guide to Indigo Children* (see Appendix E).

Cultivating Children's Intuition

Children are naturally intuitive and brave, but misunderstanding or controlling parents can hurt or even crush their innate wisdom. They thrive in an environment free of judgment and filled with trust, acceptance, and open-mindedness.

Let's look at some rituals to cultivate children's intuition and to foster their already strong connection with the Divine.

Daytime Rituals

Beyond prayer, there are many ways children can celebrate the angels in their life:

- Dancing
- Singing
- Angel-themed parties
- Art projects

The angels, Archangels, and Spiritual Support Team can give children guidance, protection, and inspiration. Children often learn through the creative process, which can be a direct channel between them and the spiritual realm. Any positive expression should be encouraged. It's also important to remind children that the angels aren't limited to their room, their imagination, or their favorite time of day. Indeed, their angel friends are with them day and night, accompanying them wherever they choose to go.

Bedtime Rituals

Nightmares are common among children, especially with their bright, vivid, and broad imaginations. You can soothe them by letting them know their guardian angels are watching and protecting them while they sleep. They will not let anything harm them.

It helps to create a bedtime ritual with your children. There are many methods to help your child get a peaceful evening's rest:

- Praying to God and the angels

- Singing joyful songs

- Telling angelic stories

- Creating guided imagery meditations

The latter, creating guided imagery meditations, is worth discussing more. In short, you can help your child visualize angelic protection from harm. Tell them to close their eyes, and then help them imagine the sweet angels coming into their room, tucking them in, and standing watch from anything that may disrupt their important rest that night.

Angels 101

If they have nightmares or scary visions while sleeping, remind children that they can call Archangel Michael for safety and protection before they go to sleep.

Home Environment

Negative energy at home affects everyone, particularly children who are sensitive and intuitive. It may not be possible to create the perfect environment, but try to shield children from the following negative expressions:

- Fears and phobias

- Excessive worry

- ◆ Explosive anger

- ◆ Abusive arguments

- ◆ Frequent judgments and blame

Conflicts do happen, and the heavy energy can be broken up in several ways:

- ◆ Releasing pleasant smells a la aromatherapy

- ◆ Taking flower essences

- ◆ Using singing bowls

- ◆ Ringing a bell in each corner of each room

- ◆ Clapping throughout the house

- ◆ Playing gentle music

- ◆ Avoiding clutter and disorganization

- ◆ Designating certain areas of the house as quiet or meditative zones

- ◆ Dancing and singing with your child or children

Singing bowls, aromatherapy, and flower essences are discussed in depth in Chapter 5.

Imaginary Friends

When a child speaks of an invisible playmate, it is not always an imaginary friend. Many children have a highly functioning sixth sense, and it is wise not to simply dismiss what the child says as make-believe. Pay attention to what the child tells you and ask lots of questions. Sometimes the imaginary friends are spirits or angels. Other times your child's heightened sense of intuition may be picking up on something, such as a baby you lost in childbirth or a child who was given up for adoption.

Cecily's Childhood Friend

Many children often just know things. Their intuition is wide open because they do not yet hold preconceived notions or fears about the information their spiritual antennae has picked up.

Cecily found this in her own life, yet she had to wait until she was almost 30 years old before she could recognize and validate her own intuitive antennae in action during childhood.

For a good year or two in childhood, Cecily had an imaginary companion named Joe Bert. Joe Bert was her older brother and they were very close. In fact, the only time he wasn't by her side was when he would go off and play chess. Cecily spoke of Joe Bert on a daily basis to her mother, and she was always game to include him in their lives.

In her adulthood, Cecily found out that she had an older brother with the same parents that was given up for adoption. After many years of wondering about the sibling she didn't know, Cecily found him in 1999 and it was a joyous reunion. Luckily, his name did not turn out to be Joe Bert, because that would be just too much synchronicity for one day!

The Least You Need to Know

- ◆ Children have a special relationship with the angels because they just left the spirit realm and are more open-minded than adults.

- ◆ Children can identify with a certain animal to increase self-esteem, courage, and feelings of security.

- ◆ Indigo Children are super-sensitive, intuitive kids who will usher a new age into the world.

- ◆ Daytime and nighttime rituals can help kids feel more at one with the angels and aid them with sleeping.

- ◆ Imaginary friends may not be imaginary at all, but representative of their spirit guides or the angels.

Chapter 12

Relationship Angels: Soulmates and Twin Flames

In This Chapter

- ◆ Understanding soulmates
- ◆ Building positive relationships with angelic assistance
- ◆ Learning about twin flames
- ◆ Learning whether you are destined to be together
- ◆ How Archangel Chamuel helps soulmates meet
- ◆ What to expect from a soulmate connection

The common belief is that falling in love is always a natural and easy process. Unfortunately, between our busy schedules, our often negative attitudes, and our sometimes isolating modern world, it can be difficult to create and explore healthy and lasting romantic interests—or to maintain the love relationships we already have.

Here's another area where you can call on your angels for help. The angels are amazing at being supportive of our relationships, both established and flourishing.

What Is a Soulmate?

The angels are a wonderful resource for finding the love life we desire. Many of us are searching for our *soulmate*. In our culture, the soulmate ideal has long been the relationship we all covet. But what really is a soulmate? In some ways, the whole perception of a soulmate is one of the most misunderstood terms in modern history.

def•i•ni•tion

A **soulmate** is a partner and helper with whom we share many life lessons and similar soul development.

First, let's explore the ins and outs of the soulmate concept. Then we can look at how the angels can help us connect with them!

The Soulmate Ideal

Many people truly believe or at least hope that the perfect romantic partner is out there: someone who is a lock to his or her key, a yin to his or her yang—a companion who matches in both mind and spirit. Essentially, they are looking for their ideal complement. The comforting fact is that most people are looking for his or her soulmate as well. We have a human longing to unite and become one with another.

Not unlike trying on a pair of jeans, the search for a romantic soulmate might be compared to finding just the right fit. Some will be too tight, others too loose. However, if you are lucky, you'll walk in the store and *immediately* find the right pair. Other times you spend the greater part of the day going store to store, not quite finding the right fit until later that evening or, perhaps, on another shopping day. It all depends on synchronicity—that is, the right timing.

The way it's used in everyday talk, it's easy to assume a soulmate is a person with whom you're madly in love. Yet this common belief is a bit of a misnomer. In truth, a soulmate can be a lover, husband, or wife, but can also be a mother, brother, or another family member; your best friend; or even a teacher or mentor. In other words, your soulmate need not be someone with whom you form a romantic relationship. It's about a strong, unique soul connection that has lasted during several lifetimes together.

Enlightenments

Relationships can end, of course, but that doesn't mean that our former lover, partner, or friend isn't one of our soulmates. Sometimes people have to spend time apart to finish learning their life's lesson. In other cases, our relationship has to evolve into something else to progress, whether it's a teacher turning into a colleague or a girlfriend turning into a wife. The growing pains in between are necessary to move the relationship to its next level and to begin learning more spiritual lessons.

It's possible to have multiple soulmates. They all serve a different purpose in our lives, as we do in theirs. For instance, a thoughtful soulmate may help us become more patient in love, while a spontaneous, funny soulmate may help us take life less seriously. It's a mutual bond, so you may help the thoughtful soulmate be more assertive or help the spontaneous, funny soulmate stay more focused and disciplined.

Some soulmate relationships are based on past karma. Some are not. As an example, you could reconnect with a person whom you mistreated in some form in the last life. In this life, you may help them heal in some way, while they learn to forgive you in some form. We're not privy to these details—after all, we're human—but we can communicate with the angels to guide us toward making the right decisions. For nonkarmic or companion soulmates, our relationship is a lot simpler—there is little to no built-up karma, nothing to balance, and nothing to correct. With a companion soulmate, we can build our relationship in the here and now and enjoy the support and joy that comes with it.

A Soulmate Helps You Grow

As humans, we often think that challenging relationships are bad— therefore, our relationship with someone who could be our soulmate should be smooth sailing from the get-go. That's not necessarily true.

You might say that this is an idealized notion of what a soulmate relationship should be like.

In fact, the purpose of a soulmate is to help us grow, just as our purpose in their lives is to help them grow. Growth can be hard. Hence, the people we are closest to can be the very people that cause us the most frustration!

> **Advice from Above**
>
> There is a difference between a challenging, growth-filled partnership and a toxic, abusive relationship. Make sure that the people in your life are supportive and loving of who you are and are equally supportive of who you can become.

Many of our most important relationships were already decided before we were born. Before birth, we agreed to be helpful to our soulmates by ...

- Guiding them toward particular life lessons.
- Providing focus for their higher goals and ideals.
- Being in their lives for a particular amount of time.
- Allowing them to guide us as much as we guide them.

The challenge is we don't always want to hear what is best for us. After all, if we didn't need support and guidance on our life's journey, we wouldn't need soulmates—we'd walk alone on our earthly path.

The Angels Helping the Single and the Paired

We need to trust the Universe. This means trusting the guidance of the angels. Our angels already know what we need and how we need it. Also, because they know us so well, they often know the very best time for us to receive what we long for. Through their infinite wisdom, they see your relationships in the perfect form and know in what ways you need to change—and grow—to help create this perfect union. Through their eyes, you can see opportunity in setbacks and lessons in challenges.

If we're single, the angels can help us find a soulmate who complements our own personal strengths and gifts. The key is to express what you want while trusting that the Universe will give you what you need.

If we're in a soulmate relationship, the angels can help us find perspective and see the bigger picture of love, balance, and peace. They push us to the next level of expression in our expression of joy and our capacity to love.

Twin Flames vs. Soulmates

Twin flames are often mistaken for soulmates, and, after you learn of them, it will be easy to see why. Both twin flames and soulmates have a deep, intimate connection.

The key difference is that while soulmates can represent a lifelong partnership, twin flames are two individuals who need each other to reach a specific goal.

For instance, a soulmate may be someone who becomes your lover and best friend. You share dinners, travel together, blend your lives— all those great, intimate things that we receive from our partners. However, you and your partner may not create a wonderful piece of art together, or make a great scientific discovery by pushing each other to work harder in the lab. Excellent companionship, support, and personal growth aside, the function of a soulmate relationship is much less purpose-driven.

> **def•i•ni•tion**
>
> A **twin flame** is a person who has the qualities you need to accomplish a great goal. They need you as much as you need them.

A twin flame relationship is quite different. The purpose of a twin flame is that you both need each other to accomplish a specific aim or mission—together. You push each other to achieve more than you probably could have individually.

We're not saying that soulmate relationships are less meaningful or important, but that twin flame relationships are often a means to an end. Soulmate relationships are perfectly functional without an overriding goal or desire. On the other hand, twin flame relationships can "burn out" after the mission is accomplished.

Waiting on a Fantasy

Soulmate relationships are magical, as there is usually a particular time—a unique moment—when both people realize that they are indeed soulmates. This is what makes them beautiful, as soulmate recognition requires little to no effort on our part. We just know that this person is who we are meant to share our lives with. This immediate understanding is natural, comfortable, and instinctive. The only real requirement is faith that the soulmate is out there and that you will meet him or her at the perfect time in both your lives.

Ironically, idealism can become our worst enemy when it comes to soulmates. For instance, do you ever pine for an old love, believing you were meant to be with him or her? Or do you ever get the feeling that you and another person would be the perfect couple—if that person wasn't already married to someone else?

It's human nature to believe that we're destined to be with someone, but there is a great deal of safety in believing our destiny belongs with someone *who isn't available.* It is much easier to pine after what isn't available than to deal with real people, real romantic opportunities, and real risks to be taken. It is easier to play it safe.

You have no idea what your life would be like if you did stick with your old love—and you certainly cannot go back in time to find out—nor do you know what it would be like to be married to a close, already married friend. It is beyond your understanding.

However, what is best for us is not beyond the understanding of our angels. We can block angel blessings—and a soulmate connection—when we do not trust the process. By daydreaming about a fantasy love we cannot have, a wonderful opportunity might pass us by. It also makes us seem ungrateful for all the blessed relationships our angels already have given us.

Calling on the Angels

The angels want you to be the best, happiest person you can be, and because soulmates are key to the equation, they would like nothing more than for you to connect with the right people. Furthermore, they can not only help you connect with future soulmates, but mend and re-establish your bond with current soulmates in your life. They also provide healing, guiding you toward emotional peace after a break-up and helping you trust another person again when the time is right to move on to another relationship.

Enlightenments

From the angels to soulmates, we're always surrounded by support. Notice a pattern here? We are never alone, and love is always available from our spiritual onlookers, our cheerleaders from beyond, or our flesh-and-blood friends here on Earth.

Archangel Chamuel

Archangel Chamuel is the Archangel of soulmates. As you may remember from Chapter 3, Archangel Chamuel is a champion of empathy, relationships, and healing. His main service is to develop a conscious sense of gratitude to the Source and to expand the love of one's heart to include others.

Not sure how to start your communications with Archangel Chamuel? Here is a prayer Cecily recommends:

> Archangel Chamuel, please give me the guidance to attract my soulmate to me. Help me open my heart to the heart of another, so I may experience true and lasting love. Aid me in overcoming fears and blocks that I have developed from past experiences and relationships. Give me the patience to wait for the divine timing when I can meet my partner that possesses the qualities that I hold dear. Thank you.

Romance Angels

Aside from Archangel Chamuel, there are many other angels to call upon. Open up your heart and feel free to speak to these additional heavenly helpers:

- ◆ The Angel of Attraction
- ◆ The Angel of Divine Partnership
- ◆ The Angel of Love
- ◆ The Angel of Marriage

The angels also can direct you to earthly help. An angelic prayer may lead you to a counselor who understands you and/or your soulmate's needs, a workshop that helps take your relationship with yourself or your partner to the next level, or to energy work that balances your rhythm so that you may meet or get along better with your soulmate.

The Angels and the Law of Attraction

The angels want us to be aware of and work with the law of attraction—the idea that we create our own life circumstances through our thoughts, our beliefs, and of course our actions—even those that we're not conscious of. In short, what we send out into the Universe comes back to us. This is one of many important *Spiritual Laws*.

Each thought and belief we have holds a unique energy that, similar to a magnet, draws to us similar energy in the form of our experience.

def•i•ni•tion____

A **Spiritual Law** is one of several fundamental spiritual truths that exist and function in the Universe.

If we focus on harmony and send out peaceful thoughts each day, our reality will be drama-free except for those specific soul lessons we must learn. Likewise, if we send out thoughts of the world being against us, it will most certainly seem that way.

How does this apply to your soulmates? Well, all the people we attract into our life are there as an exact reflection of the energy we hold. If we hold a belief that we only attract losers, we will attract people that perpetuate this belief. And regardless of how much the higher powers would like to give us the best, Spiritual Law dictates that we only receive what we desire consciously or unconsciously.

Your mindset and beliefs actually affects who enters—and stays—in your life. As a simple example, let's say you are truly afraid of being alone. That fear may make you cling to someone who isn't worthy of your love when, because of the commitment, you miss an opportunity to connect with a soulmate. Alternatively, you may end a beneficial relationship early because you're afraid that the person will leave you first.

These are just examples, but most of our negative energy stems from one principle mistake: we don't believe we're worthy of true love. The angels know we all deserve to be loved for who we are—warts and all—and are therefore happy to help us on our individual journeys toward positive relationships.

> **Angels 101**
>
> The angels can actually help you meet the soul of your partner on a higher plane before you meet that person here on Earth. Practice meditating, picturing both your heart and your soulmate's heart, and visualize the two combining into one energy.

Furthermore, it is important to be patient with the process. We want to put our energy out there—asking for a soulmate, wanting to heal our current relationships—and get immediate healing. It may not work like that.

When we work with the Universe, we must have the patience to trust *divine timing*. People will enter our lives exactly when they should. As you probably have witnessed, some folks married their high school sweethearts and stayed happily together for the rest of their lives. For other people, they might not meet their soulmate until they are in their 40s, 50s, or even older. It takes faith to trust that our spiritual helpers, the angels, and the Archangels have our best interest in mind.

> **def•i•ni•tion**
>
> **Divine timing** is when the Universe coordinates an event at the perfect moment for all parties involved.

What to Expect from a Soulmate

Focusing the right energy into your love relationships is key to drawing a soulmate into your life, but what happens when you actually meet him or her? It's important to have the highest intention and clarity both before and after the connection.

Focus on What You Want

Negativity breeds negativity. The Universe responds best to positive thoughts. Think about it: isn't it easier to take action when you're told what needs to be done versus only what you *shouldn't* be doing?

It may be initially easier to say "I don't want a partner who limits my creativity," but it is much better to put out there "I want a partner who will fuel my creativity and help me soar!"

There are many positive affirmations to send into the Universe and to your angels when you want to meet a soulmate. Here are a few:

◆ I want a soulmate who will accept me for who I am.

◆ I want a soulmate who will make me strive to be a better person.

◆ I want an equal in my life.

◆ I want to be the best companion possible to my soulmate.

It's easy to think positive, affirming thoughts when we long for a soulmate, but we can be quick to forget about and appreciate those we already have in our lives. Relationships can be tough, and it's easy to take loved ones and other relationships for granted. Positive affirmations can be applied to any major relationship, whether they are deep, romantic soulmate commitments, family relations, or co-workers at your job.

Here are positive affirmations to the angels for our current relationships:

◆ I believe my soulmate is doing the best he or she can every day.

◆ I believe my relationship with my soulmate will improve in every way.

◆ I believe my soulmate is worthy of my love, as I am worthy of his or hers.

◆ I believe we have a soulmate connection for a reason.

Release the Need to Save Others

Although we all have the potential to be selfish—only thinking of what we can get out of a relationship—we also have the opposite danger of creating imbalanced relationships where we keep giving without getting much in return from our partner.

We sometimes are drawn to needy people because, as long as the focus remains on them, we never have to feel vulnerable or needy ourselves. In the end, however, our deeper needs for equality and love are never met in these lopsided relationships.

All the angels, Spiritual Support Team, and Archangels do not want you to be a martyr for another person. Soulmate love is not only about loving another, but having a relationship where you can easily love yourself.

Set Realistic Expectations

Finally, although there is something magical and beautiful about connecting with another soul on a spiritual level, it's important to know that your soulmate is human—just like you.

Because it's a human relationship, your soulmates may …

◆ Accidentally hurt your feelings.

◆ Do things that drive you crazy.

◆ Say the wrong things.

◆ Disappoint you.

As we mentioned earlier, these people are soulmates because they complement your life in certain ways. The growth that comes with soulmate relationships can be challenging, frustrating, and patience-testing.

Soulmate relationships are also mystical, rewarding, and fulfilling in ways that many relationships are not. The angels certainly believe that it is worth the trouble—which is why they want to help you connect with as many soulmates as possible within your lifetime.

Write Down Your Needs

It's important to think about what you need in terms of a soulmate, but writing it down takes things to the next level. It's like a physical manifestation of our needs, and by writing it down, we're making a solid declaration to the Universe and, just as importantly, to ourselves.

Here are some steps to putting down your love desires:

1. Ask your angels to help you on your journey to find your soulmate.

2. Buy a journal especially for your soulmate notes, one to which you are "drawn."

3. Think of the qualities you want your partner to have.

4. Write one quality on each page.

5. After written, concentrate and read through each page three times.

6. Ask the angels to fulfill your wish.

7. Trust the angels, believe in divine timing, and let it go.

8. Thank your angels.

> **Angels 101**
>
> Make the process of seeking a soulmate your own. For instance, you can make a ritual or celebration by lighting a candle, burning incense, or inviting friends over for a special ceremony. We will talk more about rituals and ceremonies in Chapter 13.

One Personal Journey: Finding a Soulmate

Here are those steps in action. When Cecily began looking for a soulmate to marry and start a family with, she asked her angels to assist.

When they answered, they told her to buy a journal—not just any journal, but one that jumped out at her in the store. She did. Then the angels instructed her to think of all the qualities that she wanted her partner to possess. They guided her to write a quality on the top of each page of the journal, leaving the remainder of the page blank. Cecily continued to write down the qualities until she could think of no more. Cecily then read through each page three times and consciously gave her wish to the angels to take care of. With a sense of peace, Cecily went about her life knowing that the angels were bringing her closer to her soulmate.

Within six months, Cecily went on vacation and met her future husband, Todd. He had all the qualities she had written down. A few years later they were married and, as of this writing, are expecting their first child together.

Enlightenments

The biggest key to finding a soulmate? Actually believing that he or she exists and will appear in your life.

The Least You Need to Know

◆ Soulmates represent a deep partnership throughout your life, which can be romantic, familial, or platonic.

◆ Twin flames are similar to soulmates, but their main focus is on a mutual, specific goal as opposed to on mutual life lessons.

◆ Archangel Chamuel is the Archangel of soulmates and relationships.

◆ Relationships are based on Spiritual Law—you draw people to you based on the energy you put out.

◆ Focus on the soulmate relationship qualities you want instead of those qualities you don't.

Chapter 13

Ceremony and Ritual

In This Chapter

- ◆ The importance of ceremonies and rituals
- ◆ Using rituals to embrace and celebrate life changes
- ◆ Connecting with the angelic world through ritual
- ◆ Creating your own angel altar

From praying before every meal to meditating once a day, ceremonies and rituals help us establish sanity and stability in a seemingly unstable world. They may not magically transform the outer, material world, but their true purpose is to provide us with positive focus and inner peace.

They also can give us the clarity to better connect with our angels.

Understanding Ceremonies and Rituals

Our ancestors and the people of the world have lived with a focus on *rituals* and *ceremonies*. Think for a second about your own family traditions. Why, during the ages, have we been consistently focused on set practices?

def•i•ni•tion

A **ritual** is a set routine that brings comfort or helps keep order. A **ceremony** is a special ritual, often involving multiple persons, that honors a person or people, a spirit or spirits, or a particular life-changing event.

Aside from the security of routine, rituals create a focus—a meditation—ideal for modifying our lives. Spiritual teacher Dr. W. Brugh Joy once said that "There's a part of your psyche that doesn't know the difference between a ritual and an actual event." For example, if you take a ritual bath with the intention of purification, there is a part of you that thinks you have indeed purified yourself and can now begin anew.

Rituals have no power by themselves—they need your energy and intention to make them work. As a great catalyst for concentration and focus, rituals help your desires manifest in real life.

A Ritual Can Be Any Routine

The term "ritual" sounds kind of weird and mystical, doesn't it? However, all cultures, from African countries and Hawaiian regions to aborigines and Native Americans participate in their own special ceremonies. Think of baptisms, bar/bat mitzvahs, baby showers, and weddings. Rituals are not a pagan phenomenon, but a Universal phenomenon.

By definition, rituals have certain guidelines established by the people involved. However, what the ritual encompasses is totally up to the participants.

Remember that the power of a ritual comes from its significance and effectiveness with you personally—not from judgments of others who deem it worthy or not worthy. For instance, going to church every Sunday is a ritual for millions worldwide. Ideally, this ritual is effective for every person participating. Who is to say that praying amongst others in an organized church once a week is less or more effective than, say, regularly attending a synagogue or kneeling toward Mecca five times daily? All that matters is the impact on the individual or group doing the ritual.

That said, your ritual to connect to the spirit world can be composed of anything, from dance and spoken word to music and elaborate props. The important thing is to help you feel one with the angelic realm. Rituals have the ability to uplift your heart; lighten your emotional load; and help you feel gratitude, hope, joy, and grace again.

Advice from Above

Rituals fueled by negative intentions can create harmful energy and results. Rituals and ceremonies should never be used to hurt others.

Focus on Connecting, Not Superficial Elements

Although it's important to establish what makes the ritual feel good to you—complete darkness, special brands of candles, mood music, and so on—you mustn't become distracted by the tiny details. A ritual can be as stunning as a Shakespearean play but lack any real substance. In other words, the action has to be a means to an end.

Barbara Biziou, author of *The Joy of Ritual* (see Appendix E), calls the different parts of a ritual "ingredients." As with any recipe, you want to make sure your ingredients mesh well and all get you closer to your desired experience.

The desired end result is that you feel closer to the Divine, not that you just perform an elaborate, fancy ritual to show off to friends or as a form of creative expression. It is important not to lose sight of the true purpose of your ceremony.

Angels 101

Cultural anthropologist Angeles Arrien recommends three ways to create blessings through ritual. One is to pray every day, setting a sacred intention. Two, give gratitude every day, keeping your heart open and allowing yourself to be a student. Finally, make a life-affirming action every day—an anonymous act of kindness—to restore delight and magic into our world.

Understanding Altars

A way to pay homage to helpful angels, creating an angel altar can help you feel even more connected to the spiritual Universe. It can be centering and calming, providing you a respite from a sometimes chaotic world. The ritual takes you away from a busy schedule, and the altar and its items help you reflect and hone your concentration on Spirit.

The angels will love it, too, because you are creating a sacred space to honor your relationship with them. The ritual tightens the bonds and makes it easier for you to see, hear, and feel angelic guidance.

What Is an Altar?

An altar is a raised structure or space that serves as a sacred, intimate environment for worship and ceremony. Here we're talking about an altar within your house or on your property. It's a place where you can concentrate, get centered and heal, and also celebrate and honor holidays and special events. It can be as elaborate as a built area or as simple as a mantel.

An altar is also the place to honor life transitions, dramatic changes, and rites of passages. Consider all the shifts we deal with as humans in everyday life:

- Births
- Deaths
- Changing of the seasons
- Graduations
- Career changes
- Marriages and other commitment ceremonies
- Moving to a new home

An altar can provide a refuge or a focal point during life's major transitions. Within a family, it's a reminder to honor the past, present, and future family members.

In fact, just being in the presence of an altar can be enough to create a positive influence. The items placed within the altar itself physically represent abstract ideas, giving form to the formless, and gives us a concrete, visual connection to the spirit world. In short, an altar is a physical expression of a spiritual concept.

Enlightenments

Altars are a part of our everyday lives and nomenclature. For instance, instead of saying getting married, we will often say "going to the altar."

Altars are not only a place to center during times of joy, but also during times of sorrow. Don't be afraid to use your altar to help you find peace during difficult moments in your life.

Where to Put an Altar

Beyond our own security, an altar makes it easier for us to connect with the world of spirit. We honor our angels and guides with the creation and blessings of an altar.

To create an altar, find a small, nice corner on your property. It could be an intimate nook in your apartment, a cozy area of your house's living room, or a beautiful spot in your garden.

Adding Items to Your Angel Altar

Think about what you'd like to add, as each Earth property has a different energy. For instance, the smell of a particular flower triggers a particular spiritual, not to mention physical influence, as would an inspiring picture or a beautiful array of colors. And similar to *alchemy*, these different symbolic gestures blend into one solid theme—a particular energy—that vibrates from your altar.

def•i•ni•tion

Alchemy is the ancient art of combining materials (often chemical) to create something more valuable than the original items are separately. The practice hit peak popularity in the Middle Ages when magicians and scientists alike searched for the correct items to turn lead into gold.

When thinking about what to add to an altar, angel figurines are wonderfully symbolic of the spiritual beings, as are written prayers and angelic pictures. Putting fresh flowers, aromatic candles, and ripe fruits on the altar creates a strong symbol for joy and happiness. Colors also influence the energy and flow of your altar. See Chapter 10 for more about what each color represents.

Also consider stones and gems for your altar, as their earthly energy can give a grounding influence and can help you feel more centered at the altar. Some stones are also connected to other spiritual aspects. For instance, emerald, the beautiful sparkling gem, is associated with the fourth chakra, the heart chakra.

Here are some stones and gems to consider:

- Amber—To provide protection and to heal
- Amethyst—To expand compassion and intuition
- Citrine—To clear the mind
- Diamond—To inspire courage and clarity
- Emerald—To heal emotionally and spiritually
- Jade—To increase wisdom
- Lapis—To open up intuition
- Moonstone—To balance emotions
- Onyx—To help become grounded
- Quartz crystal—To create spiritual attunement
- Ruby—To revitalize health and passion
- Sapphire—To inspire devotion and dedication
- Topaz—To open up new levels of knowledge and wisdom
- Turquoise—To create balance and harmony

Enlightenments

Many healers believe that quartz crystal is one of the most powerful rocks. Known to transform energy, quartz crystal creates a sense of peace in individuals as well as environments.

As with stones and gems, plants and flowers add specific qualities and harmonies to your angel altar:

◆ Daffodil—To give innocent, youthful joy

◆ Daisy—To promote innocence

◆ Jasmine—To inspire beauty

◆ Lily—To provide purity

◆ Lily of the Valley—To help start a new beginning

◆ Lotus—To open up enlightenment

◆ Rose—To inspire love

◆ Sunflower—To revitalize optimism and positivity

◆ Tulip—To promote vitality

Advice from Above

Plant experts say Lily of the Valley can be dangerous to touch, so use care when handling it or any other plant not commonplace. It is well worth doing a quick Internet search before scavenging on your own.

There are many other items to further refine the altar. Here are some more to keep in mind:

◆ Bells—Symbolic of the soul

◆ Feathers—Symbolic of angelic flight

◆ Metals—Gold and silver represent the sun (masculine) and moon (feminine) energy

◆ Shells—Increases protection, compassion, and spiritual attunement

Enlightenments

For ages mathematicians have believed that the design of certain objects creates a "golden ratio," a measurement that connects all things found in nature. The first major proponent of the golden ratio was the ancient Roman Pythagoras, later famous for his geometric theorem. Spiritualists see the golden ratio as the fingerprint of God—a perfect number found throughout nature. Modern-day mathematicians see the golden ratio, which is 1.6180339887, in the notes of music, the Egyptian pyramids, plants, and sea shells.

There are many other items to consider for an altar, including sacred candles, holy beads, crosses, and incense. Open your mind—and your heart—and add items that feel important to you.

Using Your Altar

Before you settle in to your altar area, turn off your cell phone, put your pets in another room, and make sure the kids are settled. The goal is to set up a quiet space—one without loud noises or distractions.

Once you feel good about your altar environment, it is time to use it to connect or reconnect with your angels. Use the guided imagery exercises in Chapter 7, or pray, meditate, write in your journal, reflect, celebrate ... whatever you feel best expresses your gratitude.

Ritual is about taking a specific time each day, week, or month to honor life events. The more often you enjoy the ritual, the more comfortable and effective it will become.

The Least You Need to Know

- Rituals are nondenominational and can be as simple or as fancy as you like.

- The purpose of a ritual or ceremony is to get closer to the Divine.

- An altar is an intimate, often small area located inside your home or in the garden.

- Altars can be used to celebrate or honor major as well as minor life events—both challenging (as with death) or exciting (as with birth).

- Rocks, gems, plants, flowers, and other items blend to create a specific altar theme and energy.

14

Tapping into Your Inner Angel

In This Chapter

- How angelic qualities enrich our lives
- The top 10 qualities that help you tap into your inner angel
- What Archangels to call on to assist you in finding your divine attributes
- Questions that help you access your angelic self
- The lasting gift of angelic guidance

In today's society, the mere idea of living up to an "angelic" persona can leave 99.5 percent of the population feeling out of their league, not to mention most are not looking to be another Mother Teresa.

Yet finding our inner angel does not entail countless sacrifices, untold purity of heart and body, or putting everyone else before ourselves. It simply means tapping into the beautiful qualities and high vibration of the angels to make our lives easier and more meaningful.

Ten Basic Principles

The angels aspire to get us in touch with these innate, higher gifts and traits that we already possess on a deeper, spiritual level. When we open ourselves to angelic guidance, there are several light-filled and heavenly qualities that are readily accessible to us. We simply need to peel some layers of resistance to reveal our own divine nature.

Truth

> "No pleasure is comparable to standing upon the vantage ground of Truth."
> —Sir Francis Bacon, fifteenth-century British philosopher, statesman, and author

Truth can be found when there is no fear or shame around who you are. Acceptance in yourself and beliefs give you the courage to be "real" with those around you. "Realness" comes from spiritual wisdom and love for the self. It is not putting yourself below or above others—simply living in the now. Living in the present with self-love will shine light on your personal truth and make you more aware of Universal truths.

Living in truth means *authenticity*. Being authentic means being true to your feelings and true to yourself. We often dilute or bury our feelings to avoid confrontations. When we do not let others know our true feelings, we often find that we become frustrated and resentful and this can backfire by affecting our own health and state of mind. Authenticity means speaking our truth, in a nonjudgmental and nonabusive way, straight from the heart and spirit.

def•i•ni•tion

Being **authentic** reflects that the thoughts and emotions we express have genuinely and honestly been experienced.

Find ways to trust, love, and forgive yourself for better authenticity.

Call on Archangel Michael to help you with tapping into truth. Ask yourself these questions:

- ◆ Where have I been afraid to be truthful with myself?
- ◆ Where have I been afraid to be authentic with others?

◆ What feelings am I not fully addressing?

◆ How have my relationships been affected by me not always speaking my truth?

◆ When did I speak my truth and feel closer to others because of it?

◆ What would my life be like if I lived from a place of true authenticity?

Compassion, Love, and Service

"The best way to find yourself is to lose yourself in the service of others."
—Mahatma Gandhi, twentieth-century major political and spiritual leader of India

Compassion is what fuels us to be in service—one of our missions here on Earth. Compassion is not feeling sorry for others but relating as one human being to another—as one of God's children to another. Knowing that life can be difficult, there is no pretense in compassion as you are simply feeling and recognizing the pain of fellow brothers and sisters in our world. Compassion allows you, if just for a moment, to be in someone else's shoes. It keeps all human beings on a level playing field, as no one's life is completely charmed.

Enlightenments

Compassion and empathy are often thought to be the same thing. Not so. Compassion is more a big-picture emotion, while empathy is more situational. Compassion represents a desire to alleviate the overall pain, stress, or suffering of another, while empathy happens more in the moment in the form of a loving reaction to someone's pain. An example of empathy is feeling troubled or being helpful when you see someone crying or visibly scared. An example of compassion would be feeling concern when you find out that your co-worker is battling an incurable illness.

Self-love and compassion equal an opportunity to feel great depths of love for the people around you. Essentially, you feel a whole new level of connection with others, and the love and compassion you emanate can become contagious.

Compassion is a quality that allows us to help our fellow man and is a catalyst for getting past our obsessive focus on our own needs, worries, and ego. To experience lack of compassion comes from a me-centered belief system that ultimately comes from fear. When we focus on pleasing ourselves above everyone and everything, it is often a defense to keep out the possibility of pain, humanness, and emotion.

Things such as shut-off or numbed emotions, not yet knowing the joy of helping, and being afraid of ending up like the people in need can all be deterrents that keep a person from learning compassion, service, and unconditional love for others. Yet true wisdom and satisfaction only happens when we stop living just for ourselves.

To be in service to humanity can include a neighbor, community, country, or even the world. Serving the greater good is a noble mission here on Earth and helps us recognize that we are all one and any need that exists for others ultimately affects us all in some way. Service is spiritual, puts us in the now, and keeps us with integrity.

Look at our guardian angels; they love and accept us no matter what. They do not judge us or try to change us, but show compassion for the hard times we go through. Their role is to be in service, and they project a pure, loving energy as they assist us.

Call on Archangel Chamuel and Archangel Zadkiel to help you with tapping into compassion, love, and service. Ask yourself these questions:

◆ Where have I shown compassion and love for myself?

◆ Where have I shown compassion and love for others?

◆ Where do I need to find more compassion and love in my life?

◆ How has service to others positively impacted my life?

Enlightenments

Volunteering and philanthropy not only help us feel good, but they have been shown to have substantial health benefits as well. The Corporation for National and Community Service conducted a 2007 study that shows that service to others increases one's life span, lowers the chance of depression, and can improve functional abilities.

Forgiveness

"We must develop and maintain the capacity to forgive. He who is devoid of the power to forgive is devoid of the power to love. There is some good in the worst of us and some evil in the best of us."

—Martin Luther King Jr., prominent leader in the twentieth-century American Civil Rights Movement

Forgiveness is understanding that anger, hate, resentment, and hurt are all destructive to the person who holds onto those feelings. One of our biggest and most difficult lessons is forgiveness toward others and ourselves. Forgiveness is coming from a higher understanding that there is a lesson in all personal relationships, as we are allowing for different personal histories (of the physical body and soul) and experiences and motivations in our interactions with others.

Forgiveness doesn't mean you condone injustices, mistreatment, or abuse; it simply means you are willing to look beyond the limitations of the person's human flaws and misguided actions to see the inner light of a person's soul. It is being willing to say "we do not see eye to eye, but I can love you and respect you as a fellow human being and child of God."

No good can come from being unforgiving. It clogs us emotionally and energetically and inhibits our full expression of joy. Being unforgiving is caused by the fear that we were not honored properly, yet honor must come from inside ourselves. We must not expect that the outside world will always give us what we want. We must look inside for what we desire, not to the outside.

The angels are role models in forgiveness. Every day they witness humans doing quite shocking deeds and yet they never withdraw their love or support for humankind.

Call on Archangel Chamuel and Archangel Zadkiel to help you with tapping into forgiveness. Ask yourself these questions:

◆ What have I not forgiven others for?

◆ What have I not forgiven myself for?

◆ How have I looked to others to fulfill me?

◆ How could forgiving another bring more peace to my life?

◆ Who could I forgive starting today? How will I go about doing this?

Angels 101

One of the best ways to start the forgiveness process is by writing a letter to the person you are angry or disappointed with. Be sure to get all your unexpressed feelings out. Do not send out the first draft of this letter. It serves as a cathartic process to find out what has truly hurt you and put your feelings in perspective, so you can approach the person afterward in a more centered and loving way, either in person or by sending a thoughtful, finalized version of your letter.

Faith and Trust

"Every tomorrow has two handles. We can take hold of it with the handle of anxiety or the handle of faith."
—Henry Ward Beecher, nineteenth-century prominent reformer

Faith is being able to trust that the Universe is always looking out for our best interest and that the Universe always gives us what we need at every given moment. There is a higher plan for each of us that we may not be able to see from day to day, but to know everything is in divine order and appropriate for our growth and well-being. True faith exists without promises of what tomorrow may hold, because there is a higher and divine plan for each of us. Lack of faith is brought on by fear of not being in control, living in the future, and fear of failure.

You are always choosing even when on a conscious level you do not think so, the Universe or God is never doing anything to you that you do not already want or have not already agreed to on some level.

Many people do not trust themselves and it keeps them in a prison of their own making, afraid to take risks and try new things. What holds them back is the belief that things need to be in a certain order that guarantees success before they can trust. This is not always how the Universe works. True trust in oneself does not depend on the outcome. Faith and trust work hand in hand. The angels are always fully trusting of themselves and have complete faith in the Universe. They want us to have the fullest life possible and always encourage us to embrace faith and learn trust.

Call on Archangel Raphael and Archangel Gabriel to help you with tapping into faith and trust. Ask yourself these questions:

◆ When have I had complete faith in the Universe and had my needs met?

◆ When have I had complete faith in myself and succeeded?

◆ Where has not trusting myself and the Universe held me back and kept me from taking a needed risk?

◆ Where have I looked outside myself to build faith and trust?

◆ How can I look inside myself to help gain real faith and trust?

Patience

> "When clouds form in the skies we know that rain will follow but we must not wait for it. Nothing will be achieved by attempting to interfere with the future before the time is ripe. Patience is needed."
> —The I Ching, ancient Chinese oracle

There is an old saying that goes "Good things come to those that wait." This is not always a valued mantra in today's society. Human nature is impatient—modern society accepts this. Patience comes with maturity and spiritual growth, for until we are willing to wait, we are like new-borns demanding to have our needs met. As we become more aware in our consciousness and spirituality, we learn that there is something called divine timing to everything in our lives.

What causes so many of us to be impatient? Many times when we do not get what we want right away, we become frustrated, angry, sad, or feel like a failure. Why? You might say it stems from a belief and fear that we are not in true control of our lives and may never get what we really desire.

Patience brings wisdom and trust that what we put into our lives energetically will come back to us in the right time.

Call on Archangel Gabriel to help you learn patience. Ask yourself these questions:

- How often do I expect instant gratification in my life?

- When have I pushed to receive things because I was scared I would not get my desires met?

- When has patience paid off for me?

Abundance and Grace

"Abundance is not something we acquire. It is something we tune into."
—Dr. Wayne Dyer, prominent modern-day author and psychologist

Abundance is our divine right as children of God. It is the life spring of the Universe, and we can tap into it at any time. When we are shining brightly with a high vibration, we are able to claim our God given prosperity in life. Grace is being in the flow. An effortless flow of synchronicities, joy, and blessings come when you are living in balance and harmony. It is being in the daily mindset of abundance and grace, much like an energetic tune up that brings more of what we want into our lives.

A fear of not having enough, not being good enough, or failing all play into lack of abundance and grace. The angels know better. The angels do not have to struggle to have their needs met, nor do they exist in a fearful state, because they know that the Universe has unlimited abundance for them and all they need to do is tap in.

Call on all the Archangels to help you tune into abundance and grace. Ask yourself these questions:

- Where does my current life show abundance and grace?
- Where does my current life lack abundance and grace?
- In what areas do I feel worthy of abundance?
- In what areas do I feel unworthy of abundance?
- What can I do starting today to tap in to abundance?

Serenity

"Serenity is not freedom from the storm, but peace amid the storm."
—Anonymous

Serenity is a state of body, mind, spirit, and emotion. One does not need to be in meditation or on vacation to find serenity. Even in the midst of noise or chaos, we can choose to be peaceful and calm. Serenity creates balance, less drama, and more understanding in our lives. We have more awareness and less distraction. The spiritual world is in peace. When we do not have serenity in our lives it is often because we are afraid of our own mortality. We have become addicted to chaos in self-defense—we do not need to look at ourselves and address our spirit.

Many times we take on others' problems and drama to feel more alive or to distract us from our own lives. Sometimes we enjoy it so much that we interfere in others' lives and try to change them. As a result, we find the opposite of serenity; we find conflict and hardship.

The angels find serenity in every moment, because they do not live in fear or have a need to change others or be involved in their drama. Their goal is peacefulness and steadiness.

Call on Archangel Jophiel and Archangel Chamuel to help you experience serenity. Ask yourself these questions:

- In what areas in my current life do I have serenity?

- What parts of my current life are without serenity?

- What part am I playing in my current state of serenity?

- How have I let others take away my serenity?

- What relationships (friends, family, colleagues) create the most drama in my life?

Advice from Above

Be patient with yourself as you access your divine qualities within. You do not need to be perfect, nor do you need to tap into all 10 qualities at the same time. Some will be easier for you, so don't be afraid to concentrate on those that are more natural for you first. Even small changes for the better in each area can make your life easier and happier.

Devotion and Purpose

"And the day came when the risk to remain tight in a bud was more painful than the risk it took to blossom."
—Anais Nin, twentieth-century American author

Finding our true passion in life and working hard are divine concepts. Our lives are not complete without a purpose or cause to devote ourselves to. It does not need to be grand, but we do need to be in the game of life in at least one area of daily existence (when we are not sitting on the sidelines and watching the world pass us by).

At the time of our birth, we were given unique gifts of personality, talent, and abilities plus a mission for our lifetime here on Earth. If we fall off track and get lost, we often get confused about our reason for being on Earth. Not knowing what our calling is can leave us feeling numb and unfulfilled. We must look inside ourselves to find it, and when we do, we must give of ourselves—body, heart, and soul—to be the best we can be. This is what the angels do on their mission to assist humanity.

Call on Archangel Michael to help you find devotion and purpose. Ask yourself these questions:

♦ What are my biggest passions in life?

♦ Where do I need to find more passion or interest in my life?

♦ Do I work with devotion in any areas of my life? If so, what are they?

♦ If I could have three top purposes in my life, what would they be?

Higher Understanding

"Learn to get in touch with the silence within yourself, and know that everything in life has purpose. There are no mistakes, no coincidences, all events are blessings given to us to learn from."
—Elisabeth Kübler-Ross, Swiss-American psychiatrist and author

Higher understanding is the ability to see beyond the obvious without being limited or handicapped by our experiences, past, or human limitations. It is using our intuition, perception, and awareness to see things from a higher perspective without the fear and petty concerns of everyday life.

Higher understanding comes with the realization that the Universe is working from a place that we may not totally understand at the moment, but over time we will assuredly see the divine workings of the Universe with much more clarity and appreciation.

It is the knowledge that we are learning lessons every day and even though things may seem hopeless, they never are. Through higher understanding, we gain the wisdom to know that God and the Universe do not take away from us or give us hardships and struggle.

We bring about our own challenges, for we are one with the Universal energy and our free will helps shape our lives. We must take responsibility for our circumstances through our choices. Whether staying in the flow or going against the tide, it is our choice and free will.

Call on Archangel Uriel to help you find higher wisdom. Ask yourself these questions:

♦ Where have I shown a sense of higher understanding in the last three years?

♦ How has my behavior, attitude, and beliefs shaped my current life?

♦ Where have I blamed the Universe for my struggle instead of looking at myself?

♦ How would developing my intuition serve me?

Joy

"It is never too late to have a happy childhood."
—Anonymous

Joy is a choice in life. It is also an attitude. Joy comes to us when we choose to embrace and bring more of it into our lives. The spiritual laws dictate that what we put out in the world comes back to us. When we decide to see our lives through a filter of joy and send joy to those around us, we experience more fun, lightheartedness, and bliss.

> **Angels 101**
>
> One of the best ways to experience more joy in life is by not taking things too seriously all the time. Laughter and humor are wonderful healers and powerful keys to unlocking happiness.

An important part of receiving joy is finding out what makes you happy. Through our inner child and our creative self, we are able to express our joy freely and really feel it. Look at children; they find joy effortlessly. When you are yearning for joy, simply become more childlike by being playful, acknowledging the joy you already have in your life, and living in the present moment.

The angels live in a joyful state because they have appreciation for what they already possess and do not depend on anything or anyone to make them happy. They know that happiness comes from within.

Call on all the Archangels to help you find joy. Ask yourself these questions:

◆ What things in my life do I feel good about?

◆ What are some good things in my life that I created for myself?

◆ What do I like about myself—in my body, my emotions, my mind, and my spirit?

◆ What things make me feel happy?

◆ In what areas of my life do I need to lighten up and be more playful?

A Lasting Gift

The true purpose of this book is to teach anyone who has the interest that tapping into angelic guidance becomes a treasured gift and steady support in our hectic world. From the smallest everyday tasks to the largest crossroads in our lives, the angels are available to us as a heavenly resource direct from God. In fact, the most auspicious time to get help from the angels is when we are traveling off course and moving away from our highest spiritual path. When things are just not working for us, you might say that the angels serve as a loving light and presence in the storms of our lives, helping us recognize our inborn power, courage, and deep understanding to wisely navigate through our days and get back on track. Yet the angels can also be joyous and loving companions during our happier times, encouraging us to shine our own beautiful light for others every chance we get.

As this book illustrates, any time of day is a sacred time for calling on the angels. Cecily has found that for her students, connecting with the angelic realm on a regular basis is completely life changing. Those who have made a daily ritual out of using their intuition and awareness to commune with the angels and the rest of the Spiritual Support Team benefit in so many ways—spiritually, mentally, emotionally, and physically. When the angels enter our lives, building closer relationships, finding success, and experiencing joy all become less of a struggle or mystery and more of a way of life.

The Least You Need to Know

◆ You don't need to be a saint to find angelic qualities within.

◆ The angels want to help us explore our divine qualities to have more joy and meaning in life.

◆ Each attribute has one or more Archangels assigned to it.

◆ Inspired qualities such as compassion, trust, love, and patience can all be accessed by each of us.

◆ The right questions can help us tune in to our angelic self.

A

Glossary

acupuncture   An ancient form of traditional Chinese medicine that works directly with the flow of chi. It is the practice of inserting thin needles into specific points on the body with the aim of relieving pain or for other therapeutic purposes.

aka cords   Etheric cords known in Hawaiian mysticism. They are strong strings of energy built between us and those we care about. They are only visible to the clairvoyant and felt by the clairsentient.

alchemy   The ancient art of combining materials (often chemical) to create something more valuable than the original items are separately. The practice hit peak popularity in the Middle Ages when magicians and scientists alike searched for the correct items to turn lead into gold.

altar   A raised structure or space which serves as a sacred, intimate environment for worship and ceremony. In this book, we're talking about an altar within your house or garden. It is a place where you can concentrate, get centered and heal, and also celebrate and honor holidays and special events.

angel   An eternal spiritual guide and messenger, under a higher power, sent to help humanity.

angel art Messages from the angels through drawing and coloring. The receiver uses the intuitive channels of clairvoyance, clairaudience, intuitive empathy, and clairsentience to draw various shapes and colors as a means of angelic communication. Each hue, shade, and tone carries a different meaning.

angelic shielding Creating a light-filled boundary between your energy field and the energy fields of others. These shields use high-color frequencies direct from the angelic realm.

anthropomorphism The practice of giving human characteristics to a nonhuman being or object.

apocalypse A prophecy of an end-all war or disaster. It can also mean the event itself.

apparition A phenomenon where an ethereal figure appears in an unexpected or extraordinary way.

Archangels The captains and managers of all the angelic kingdom, They are powerful beings who embody divine attributes and are in service to all of humankind.

aromatherapy Essential oils made from plants and flowers that work with the human energy field through vibrations in promoting emotional, physical, and spiritual healing.

Ascended Masters Enlightened spiritual beings who excelled here on Earth and have reconnected with God. As true teachers of humankind, their goal is to raise our spiritual evolution. Examples include Buddha, Kwan Yin, St. Germaine, and Jesus.

aura The seven subtle bodies or layers around the physical body. Each of the subtle bodies work as a team with the chakras to create our own personal energy field. *See also* chakra.

auric Anything related to the aura.

authentic Behavior or state of being that reflects that the thoughts and emotions we express have genuinely and honestly been experienced.

ceremony A special ritual, often involving multiple persons, that honors a person or people, a spirit or spirits, or a particular life-changing event.

chakra   An energy center located in the larger field of energy around our bodies. Each of the seven chakras run along the spine and affect our emotional, physical, spiritual, and mental states.

cherub   A high-ranking angel. The plural version is cherubim.

chi   Positive life force that flows from the human energy system. Chi rises from the base of the spine up through the chakras into the head center. *See also* chakra.

clairaudience   Clear hearing; the ability to hear outside the normal range of sound.

claircognizance   Clear knowing; inner knowing through thoughts, ideas, and concepts that come instantaneously.

clairsentience   Clear feeling; the ability to feel and capture information through sensations, often receiving messages through the emotions and senses.

clairvoyance   Clear seeing; our third eye chakra works in conjunction with the occipital lobe of our brain to let us see beyond the veil through visions and images.

divine timing   When the Universe coordinates an event at the perfect moment for all parties involved.

ego   The self, separate from others and the world at large. In psychoanalysis, the ego is the division of the psyche that is conscious, controls thought and behavior, and is most in touch with external reality.

elemental realm   Nature spirits that work under Mother Earth (Gaia), including fairies, gnomes, sylphs, and elves.

epiphany   A seemingly sudden insight that changes one's understanding about life or a specific situation.

flower essences   Remedies that are water-based infusions of the blossoms from a wide variety of flowers, trees, shrubs, and plants. The essences are vibrational in nature and work deeply within the human energetic field to restore balanced energy flows. Their most significant impact comes from rebalancing and transforming the emotions. These essences encourage a gentle and noninvasive clearing of stuck negative emotions by restoring energy flow and healthy vibratory frequencies in the emotional body.

free will The philosophical idea that you have the freedom to do what you want when you want without being constrained by a determined fate.

guided imagery What you see in your mind's eye. It can also include broader imagery such as what you hear, feel, smell, and taste in your imagination. This type of visualization is often led by imagery meditations in books and CDs or by a practitioner.

Immaculate Conception Often used to describe any pregnancy done without human intercourse or intervention; however, the term technically only applies to the birth of Jesus—hence the capitalization.

Indigo Children A group of ultra-sensitive and highly intuitive kids meant to take humanity to the next level.

intuitive empathy A heightened form of clairsentience that tunes into other people's emotions, energies, and illnesses.

mana A Hawaiian word for life force energy; also called chi or prana.

medium A person who professionally communicates with the spirit world. Mediums are often hired to connect the living with the deceased.

oracle cards Divination card decks with metaphysical themes, such as angelic messages or intuitive guidance. They do not contain the darker images of traditional Tarot card decks.

paradigm A framework of ideas or rules people work within. A paradigm shift is a major occurrence that shifts these ideas or rules.

philanthropy Goodwill toward others or literally giving a gift or contribution to someone in need.

Qigong The ancient Chinese art and science of becoming aware of one's life force energy and learning how to master its flow through a controlled composition of posture, movement, meditation, and breathing. The word means "breath work" or "energy work" in Chinese.

Reiki An ancient system of hands-on energy healing. The Japanese word *Reiki* means "Universal life energy." Much like other healing therapies, Reiki works with balancing and restoring the flow of chi.

ritual A set routine that brings comfort or helps keep order.

seer   A person who sees things other people cannot see easily, such as spirits or even the future.

seraph   A high-level angel; a multiwinged protector of God's throne.

serendipity   Finding things working highly in your favor without your intervention—that is, out of "coincidence."

soulmate   A partner and helper with whom we share many life lessons and similar soul development.

spirit guide   A spiritual being that has lived on Earth before and serves as a seasoned mentor.

spiritual contracts   Agreements you've made with other individuals before coming to Earth to teach, love, and guide each other. For instance, in this life your best friend may help you get organized, while you may help her be more fun and spontaneous. Those roles were already decided and agreed upon by both of you before you were born on Earth. Spiritual contracts can apply to boyfriends, wives, or even your boss. It all depends on the depth of the relationship and karmic connection between you and another individual.

Spiritual Law   One of several fundamental spiritual truths that exist and function in the Universe.

Spiritual Support Team   Spiritual helpers, spirit guides, deceased loved ones, and nature spirits that assist the angels in helping us live up to our highest potential.

spread   A collection of cards organized in a particular pattern. The term can apply to any type of cards. For instance, a full house, two of a kind, and a royal flush are poker card spreads.

synchronicity   When two seemingly separate events work in conjunction with each other. The results are usually positive.

twin flame   A person who has the qualities you need to accomplish a great goal. This person needs you as much as you need him or her.

vibration   The energetic frequency that our energetic system carries. Communicating regularly with the angels helps us keep our vibrations high and positive.

vocal toning   A simple and natural form of sound therapy that works directly on the human energetic field. A tone is a distinct vocal sound that maintains a constant pitch and vibration. In the process of toning, single tones—often vowels sounds—are sustained vocally, such as "Aaaah" or "Ooooh."

wonder   When our senses are excited by novelty, astonishment, surprise, or admiration.

Yahweh   Often used as another name for God. It literally means the God of Israel.

Appendix B

Questions and Answers

Have unanswered questions about the angels and the spirit world? Comb through the following frequently asked questions to get your answer.

Do the angels usher us into heaven when we die?

Yes, the angels are our guides when we pass over. They assist us in leaving our earthly home behind and escort us to our new home on the other side. Very often, people near death talk of angelic visitations.

I have tried to contact my angels and I never receive a message back from them. How can I get their attention?

You already have their attention! From the moment you invited them into your life, they have wanted to connect with you! The angels will always send you guidance; however, you may not be able to see it, hear it, or sense it. To better receive angelic messages, you need to practice quieting mind chatter and getting rid of distractions while tuning into the angels. Work on doing the guided meditations in this book to help calm the body, mind, and emotions to enhance your angel radar.

Does the devil exist?

Cecily has learned from her spiritual mentors and has received guidance direct from the angelic realm that evil is not the work of a devil, but a product of our own free will here on Earth. There is no one entity, such as the devil, orchestrating evil. Wickedness and criminal behavior are absolutely the choice of the perpetrator and not from outside demonic forces. Some of us choose light, while others choose darkness.

When you open your intuitive abilities, aren't you opening yourself up to dark forces?

As mentioned previously, darkness is real here on Earth and is also real in other realms through the intention and free will of souls. Yet this does not mean that when you open up your higher sensitivity to the other realms that you will find yourself at the whim of negative entities. Protective energetic shielding, positive intentions, prayers, and the calling in of the angels make our intuitive journeys beautiful, joyous, and highly beneficial.

Do mean or evil people still have guardian angels?

Yes, every person here on Earth was born with one or more guardian angels. Those that choose to be evil during their lifetime simply ignore their angels. The angels stand by in nonjudgment until a person chooses to evolve spiritually either in this lifetime or another and invites them in.

Watching a human do dark, wicked, and misguided things is difficult for the guardian angels, yet they always stay balanced, loving, and there for that person.

Why is life on Earth so hard?

You might say life is a school and each human being is a student. Each of us is here to learn certain lessons to help us remember our divine heritage. If we choose not to listen to, follow, or learn from the innate wisdom of our own highest self or the guidance of spirit, we will experience so much more pain and struggle along the way. We are not here to suffer, but our own ego, habits, and fear can often sabotage us from enjoying the kind of life we long for. With higher spiritual understanding, we are able to avoid drama, judgment, and the feeling of undeserving that often accompany our pain.

Are the angels ever born into human bodies?

Our angels have never been human before. However, there is a belief that some humans do have angelic heritage. Cecily's teacher, Doreen Virtue, believes that a small number of angels have chosen to be incarnated into the physical form during this time in history. These angelic souls are often in service professions and enjoy helping others. Natural people pleasers, they like to see the best in everyone and are extremely nurturing. You can find out more about incarnated angels in Doreen's book, *Earth Angels*.

Does my pet have guardian angels?

In the animal kingdom, guardian angels are from the elemental realm. Nature spirits accompany our beloved pets and help them stay safe. When you open your clairvoyance, you may see little glowing dots of light hovering around your animal.

What are the biggest blocks to connecting with the angelic realm?

Strong negative emotions, incessant mind chatter, fear, and a feeling of unworthiness are the biggest culprits in keeping us from receiving messages from our angels. The guided meditations and grounding techniques in this book and especially the suggestions from Chapter 5 can assist you in removing the beliefs and behaviors that block angelic guidance.

Do past mystical experiences such as out-of-body or near-death experiences enhance intuitive ability?

Yes. In fact, Melvin Morse, M.D., discusses in his book *Transformed by the Light* the relationship between those who have had out-of-body experiences (OBE) or near-death experiences and intuitive ability. When Dr. Morse conducted a study on the subject, he found that the group of adults and children who had OBEs or near-death experiences in the past had a higher rate of verifiable psychic activities than those in the control group.

I have heard that you are more apt to have a mystical experience if you take illegal or prescription drugs. Is this true?

Illegal or prescription drugs should never be used to create a mystical-type experience. Not only are many drugs bad for your health, but they do not have the power to heighten your spiritual consciousness. Drugs are a sorry substitute for actually being in the presence of the Divine.

I am interested in getting more in touch with my spiritual side. What is the first thing I can do?

Writing in a journal is an invaluable tool when you start your spiritual journey. Keep a small journal handy at all times, as you never know when you will receive unexpected guidance, inspiration, hunches, or visions.

My spiritual guides have been sending me visions lately, especially of butterflies. What does this mean?

When your third eye or clairvoyant gifts are open, do not be surprised if you receive mini movies or short visions in the form of symbols. When Cecily's third eye opened, her guides and angels often sent her beautiful visions of butterflies. The butterfly is the Universal symbol for intense transformation. A butterfly's life is symbolic of growth, change, and transformation. It starts out as a caterpillar and then through a process of change and transformation (the larva stage) the earthbound creature emerges as a beautiful winged creature finding new potential in its ability to take flight. You might say that the butterfly is in its highest state of being and wisdom. Whereas the caterpillar sees only what is on the ground, the butterfly has a clearer perspective.

Other common symbols include water for emotion, a book and pen for writing, a house to represent the soul, a baby for new beginnings or new life, and a nurse's cap or green light for healing.

Although some symbols are Universal, expect that your guides and angels will have their own special language of symbols that are personal only to you. Be patient; it may take time to learn what each symbol means.

Is it true when they say "When the student is ready, the teacher will appear"?

Yes. As we grow spiritually and look for more opportunities to gain wisdom and experience new challenges, the Universe looks for ways to assist us. Teachers are sent to us for specific areas of growth. There are teachers all around us; some come into our lives for only a short time, while others act more as mentors that stay in our lives for several months or several years. Teachers come in all forms, too. An author of a beloved book, a spiritual coach, a minister, or a wise family member are all examples of various teachers in our everyday life. Every teacher can be beneficial in her or his own way. Let's say you need help in learning to express your emotions; when the time is right, you will be drawn by synchronicity to the right person who can help you properly get in touch with your feelings for a healing.

My spiritual teacher wants me to follow everything he says without question. Does he really have my best interest at heart?

No. The more enlightened spiritual teachers realize that they are human and do not have all the answers. It is one thing to project confidence in the knowledge you have obtained, but it is quite another to not let others question that knowledge or come up with their own ideas and belief systems. You might say that this type of teacher is coming from a place of ego or control. Similar to the angels, the best teachers offer guidance and support and then stand back and let you exercise your own free will. If you find that a teacher wants to take your personal power by controlling your life or not letting you think for yourself, it is time to find another teacher!

Can I still become intuitive if I was not born that way?

We are all born with the ability to be intuitive; it is our birthright. Unfortunately, most of us are not used to flexing our intuitive muscles! You don't need to have a history of intuitive ability to tap into your intuitive gifts now. It's true that we are naturally more intuitive as children, because we have not developed any psychological or emotional blocks yet to close our third eye and chakras. However, when we are willing and invested in opening our intuitive facilities, knowledge, practice, and energetic healings and clearings can serve as wonderful catalysts to enhance clairvoyance, clairsentience, clairaudience, and claircognizance.

Some people, such as Cecily, have an instantaneous awakening of intuitive ability. This is usually a form of spiritual awakening that can happen at any time in a person's life.

I have always heard that fairies or other nature spirits are something out of a children's story and make believe. How can they be real?

You might say it is a common occurrence to mythologize those things we do not understand or comprehend with our five senses. Nature spirits have been seen and heard in every culture since the beginning of time, but only by those that have used their sixth sense or intuitive ability. Just because they cannot readily or easily be seen or heard within our limited human perception does not mean they do not exist. Remember, hundreds of years ago it was a scientific and widely accepted belief that the world was flat.

It is not up to us to convince you that nature spirits are real, but as you open yourself up to the magic of the unseen world, you may just find yourself face to face with a friendly elemental. In fact, as more people on Earth come to find the value in opening their sixth sense, books on fairies and such might finally move out of the categories of mythology and folklore and into categories such as nature, science, or spirituality where they truly belong.

I have heard that I have all the answers inside of me, but how do I know if my own internal compass is working?

It is important to follow your heart in life. You will know when you are on or off track by how you feel. When you are listening to your heart over your fears, the judgments of others, and your ego, you will be in the flow and experience more joy, synchronicities, and abundance in your daily life. Alternatively, when you are not on the right path, you will feel disconnected, frustrated, blocked, and will find life to be a struggle.

What other spiritual guides can I call on outside of those detailed in this book?

There are many guides to assist us, such as saints, gurus, ascended masters, and deities/devas.

Here are some of the more popular masters to help us in our daily life:

◆ Mother Mary—Mother of Jesus, whose apparitions have been in places such as Fatima, Lourdes, and Guadalupe. Mother Mary is a caretaker of children, a healer, and a compassionate guide.

♦ Jesus of Nazareth—The adored son of God who possesses miraculous powers. Call in Jesus to help heal illness, find faith, experience forgiveness, and to learn compassion.

♦ Saint Francis of Assisi—A Catholic saint born in the Italian town of Assisi. While alive he received a visit from Jesus and became a devout preacher of his word and love. He was also known to tame wild animals with his loving energy. His famous prayer is called the Prayer of Saint Francis. Saint Francis can assist us with the healing of animals and spiritual devotion.

♦ Saint Brigid of Ireland—A charitable and holy fifth-century Irish nun. Brigid showed a special love for the poor and less fortunate and was known for her common sense and natural leadership. Saint Brigid is celebrated throughout Ireland on February 1, a feast day known as Imbolc, the ceremonial first day of Spring. Saint Brigid can assist us in bringing about abundance, fertility, and new starts.

♦ St. Germaine—St. Germaine is actually an Ascended Master and not a traditional Catholic saint. Alive during the seventeenth and early eighteenth century, he was a wealthy and multitalented count who was known for his gifts in alchemy and his visionary intuitive abilities. Having ascended to the level of a master, he is available to guide us compassionately and lovingly to find courage, prosperity, manifestation, and life purpose.

♦ Kuthumi—An Indian spiritual leader from the nineteenth century. Kuthumi is now an Ascended Master known for his ability to bring about joy and humor. He also knows the importance of dedication to your life's mission. He is an effective guide to finding your calling and learning to enjoy life.

♦ Kwan Yin—A beloved Ascended Master from the Buddhist religion. Kwan Yin is known for her deep compassion, mercy, and kindness. She can assist us in matters of protection for mothers and children, fertility, and self-love.

♦ Paramahansa Yogananda—A twentieth-century guru from India. He was the founder of the Self-Realization Fellowship in America, a devout teacher of Kriya yoga, and author of the popular book

Autobiography of a Yogi. While alive, Yogananda was a prolific writer and speaker on spirituality, spiritual laws, and God. Call on Yogananda for healing, spiritual devotion, and daily spiritual practice.

♦ Lakshmi—An Indian moon deva of prosperity. She is known to bring good fortune, blessings, and abundance to those who seek her gifts.

♦ Ganesh—An elephant-headed Indian deity who is a patron of arts and sciences, and the deva of intellect and wisdom. Ask for guidance from Ganesh when starting a new venture or new path in life for insight and blessings.

Appendix C

Oracle Cards

Whether it is prayer or meditation, there are many ways to connect to the angels. However, one of the most valuable physical tools is oracle cards. Available in literally hundreds of types, oracle cards can be an easier, clearer way to communicate to the angels than other ways. Oracle cards can be purchased at spiritual stores, most major bookstores, and through various websites—search for keywords "oracle cards" to find resources on the Internet.

Understanding Oracle Cards

Available in decks, oracle cards can be used to receive guidance from higher vibrations—that is, from the angels. They can be read for yourself, or you can read them for another person looking for guidance and insight.

On first blush, oracle cards may seem the same as tarot cards, the famous decks that occultists use to predict the future. There are some key differences.

Focus on Positive Vibes

Tarot cards are known for having dramatic, intense imagery and messages depicting death, pain, or strife. Oracle cards, on the other hand, are directly tuned in to the angelic realm, and the visuals are positive and uplifting. The goal isn't to provoke fear or drama, but to encourage intuition and spiritual faith.

Solution Starter, Not Problem Solver

Tarot cards are used to predict the end result of situations. Oracle cards are used as communication devices with the angels, and as a result are guidance to present issues, not future situations. The angels rarely give predictions—it would go against our gift of free will—but may open up our ideas to our potential.

At the end of the day, the angels can raise our self-awareness and consciousness through oracle cards.

Spreads

There are several different ways to organize an oracle card reading. The layout is called a spread.

Here are some suggested spreads for your oracle cards.

Single-Card Spread

The simplest approach, the single-card spread is best for a fairly straightforward question.

1. Ask a clear question to yourself, either silently or out loud.

2. Shuffle the cards as you concentrate on the question.

3. Fan the cards out facedown.

4. Run your left hand over the cards until you are intuitively drawn to one card.

5. Flip it over. The card represents the answer to your question.

Three-Card Spread

More complex than a single-card spread, the three-card spread shows the evolution of an event during a brief period of time.

1. Ask a clear question to yourself, either silently or out loud.

2. Shuffle the cards as you concentrate on the question.

3. Fan the cards out facedown.

4. Run your left hand over the cards until you are intuitively drawn to one card.

5. Flip it over. The first card represents your immediate past.

6. Return to the cards and, with your left hand, select another card to which you are intuitively drawn.

7. Flip it over. This second card represents present events.

8. Return to the cards and, with your left hand, select the final card to which you are intuitively drawn.

9. Flip it over. This last card represents the potential outcome.

Seven-Card Spread

The seven-card spread is an even more detailed look at an event or situation.

1. Ask a clear question to yourself, either silently or out loud.

2. Shuffle the cards as you concentrate on the question.

3. Fan the cards out facedown.

4. Run your left hand over the cards until you are intuitively drawn to one card.

5. Flip it over. The first card represents your immediate past.

6. Return to the cards and, with your left hand, select another card to which you are intuitively drawn.

7. Flip it over. This second card represents the present events.

8. Return to the cards and, with your left hand, select the final card to which you are intuitively drawn.

9. Flip it over. This third card represents things hidden to you— overlooked or disregarded elements that are affecting the situation.

10. Return to the cards and, with your left hand, select the final card to which you are intuitively drawn.

11. Flip it over. This fourth card represents obstacles or challenges that must be overcome for the situation to progress.

12. Return to the cards and, with your left hand, select the final card to which you are intuitively drawn.

13. Flip it over. This fifth card represents your surroundings—the people, influences, and general environment.

14. Return to the cards and, with your left hand, select the final card to which you are intuitively drawn.

15. Flip it over. This sixth card represents the best course of action.

16. Return to the cards and, with your left hand, select the final card to which you are intuitively drawn.

17. Flip it over. This final card represents the outcome if the action in the sixth card is taken.

Situation Spread

The situation spread also uses a trio of oracle cards, but unlike the relatively objective three-card spread, the situation spread offers direct solutions to the potential dilemma.

1. Ask a clear question to yourself, either silently or out loud.

2. Shuffle the cards as you concentrate on the question.

3. Fan the cards out facedown.

4. Run your left hand over the cards until you are intuitively drawn to one card.

5. Flip it over. The first card represents your current attitude about the situation.

6. Return to the cards and, with your left hand, select another card to which you are intuitively drawn.

7. Flip it over. This second card represents a way to raise the vibration of the situation.

8. Return to the cards and, with your left hand, select the final card to which you are intuitively drawn.

9. Flip it over. This last card represents the missing ingredients needed for reconciliation and resolution.

Twelve-Month Spread

Broad and big picture, the 12-month spread gives an overview of the potential outcomes of the upcoming year. It could be on a birthday, an anniversary, on January 1, or any annual marker.

1. Ask a clear question to yourself, either silently or out loud.

2. Shuffle the cards as you concentrate on the question.

3. Fan the cards out facedown.

4. Run your left hand over the cards until you are intuitively drawn to one card.

5. Flip it over. The first card represents the current month.

6. Return to the cards and, with your left hand, select another card to which you are intuitively drawn.

7. Flip it over. This second card represents the next month. Place it next to the first card, at an angle that makes it look like the next step in a 12-step circle.

8. Continue intuitively drawing and placing cards until you have flipped a total of 12.

9. Review the spread. Starting with the first card, each card represents progressive months.

Highest Guidance Spread

Not as structured as other spreads, the Highest Guidance spread allows the angels to truly communicate with you as they see fit.

1. Ask "What do I need to know now for my highest good?" either silently or out loud.

2. Shuffle the cards as you concentrate on the question.

3. Fan the cards out facedown.

4. Run your left hand over the cards until you are intuitively drawn to one card.

5. Flip it over. The card represents the answer to your question.

6. Flip over additional cards until you intuitively feel the answer is complete.

Chakra Spread

More complex than a single-card spread, the three-card spread shows the evolution of an event during a brief period of time.

1. Ask "What do I need to know about my current energy field?" either silently or out loud.

2. Shuffle the cards as you concentrate on the question.

3. Fan the cards out facedown.

4. Run your left hand over the cards until you are intuitively drawn to one card.

5. Flip it over, place the card down, and with your left hand, select cards intuitively until you have a total of seven. In order, the seven cards represent:

    ◆ Root chakra: Your connection to the physical body, survival and nurturing abilities (both giving and receiving), and the relationship to the material body

    ◆ Sacral chakra: Your connection to sexuality, sensuality, and desires

- Solar plexus chakra: Your connection to the ego, confidence, and personal power

- Heart chakra: Your connection to the emotional self, self-love, compassion, and relationships

- Throat chakra: Your connection to ideas, self-expression, communication, and creativity

- Third eye chakra: Your connection to intuition, spirituality, and ideas

- Crown chakra: Your connection to the higher self and the Universe

General Tips

Oracle cards can be used right out of the box, but there are some guidelines that can help you have the most productive, accurate experience possible.

Touch Each Card

When you buy a new deck, be sure to touch each card—you want to make sure your particular energy is in the cards. Also, praying over the oracle cards before doing a reading will help open up the lines of communication even more.

Pick Up Cards with the Left Hand

Notice that we always recommend picking the card with your left hand? The left one is the intuitive hand. Use your left hand to get the most accurate responses.

Listen to the Cards

Remember that the angels are communicating what is most beneficial to you, which is not always what you want to hear! Open your mind and your heart before creating the line of communication through oracle cards—especially when doing a Higher Guidance spread that requires *you* to end the conversation.

Understand Upside-Down Cards

Did you flip over an upside-down card? A reversed card—one that is upside-down—represents a block. Something is preventing the situation or expression from moving forward.

Appendix D

Angel Field Trips

Angel-focused field trips serve as problem-solving rituals that better connect us with the angelic realm. Each trip is an adventure that takes you outside your everyday experience with the help of nature (local parks and gardens), aromatherapy, crystals, and guided imagery.

Before embarking on your field trips, remember to leave behind all electronic devices and personal distractions.

Serenity Field Trip

Reasons to take this trip: you are feeling overwhelmed, overcommitted, frazzled, drained, or confused.

We all feel hurried, hassled, and out of touch with ourselves sometimes and it's during these frantic times that we need to get back to the basics—simplicity, stillness, and spiritual connection. Through the tranquility and beauty of nature, we can breathe a sigh of relief and become rejuvenated again. Our angel guides on the journey can help us center ourselves and find our inner calm.

What you'll need:

- ◆ Comfortable clothing
- ◆ Healing stones (one or more)—amethyst, celestite, jasper

- Essential oils (one or more)—lavender, tangerine, patchouli, chamomile

- A peaceful and beautiful nature spot (scout out a garden or park)

When to start: early in the day, to enhance peacefulness throughout the day

After you are in your peaceful spot, hold your healing stone(s) in your left hand and gently breathe in the fragrance of the essential oil(s). Sit in a comfortable position and focus on each part of your body starting at your head and working your way down to your toes. Call in your angels to assist you in keeping still and relaxed. If your mind begins to wander or focus on worries or concerns, ask the angels to release the chatter of your mind so you can simply "be" in the moment.

Next, ask the angels to connect you with the grounding calmness of the earth's energy. Take 12 deep breaths in and out. With each breath, imagine pulsating blue and green energy coming up from the center of the earth and washing over you. Each time the earth's energy covers you, you become more and more at peace. You are creating a well of calming energy that you can draw from when you need it in the coming weeks.

Say "thank you" to the earth for its blessings. Notice the beauty around you: the serenity of the birds, the flowers, the sun, and the trees. Listen to the sounds of nature—the soft breeze in the trees, or the running of water. Be absolutely still and at one with the natural world around you. Enjoy the cleansing power of Mother Earth for as long as you like.

Things to remember:

- Breathe deeply

- Connect with nature

- Clear your mind and open your heart

Inner Child Field Trip

Reasons to take this trip: you are feeling too serious, too rigid, apathetic, or as though your life is overplanned.

As children, we knew how to have fun and find joy in the small wonders of life. Simple pleasures often made us squeal with delight. Without thinking much of the past or future, we often lived totally in the moment. A plain box could fuel our imagination turning the cardboard into a castle or space shuttle that provided us hours of enjoyment. Reconnecting with that childlike part of us is a basic soul need that is crucial to our happiness and well-being. Our angel guides want us to laugh, explore, and find wonder around us.

What you'll need:

♦ Comfortable clothing

♦ Healing stones (one or more)—amber, rose quartz, golden topaz

♦ Essential oils (one or more)—orange, jasmine, sandalwood

♦ A jar with a lid or medium-size pouch

♦ A place to explore in nature

When to start: morning or afternoon, to be out in daylight

Leave behind:

♦ A watch

♦ Adult concerns

Think of this excursion as a journey of discovery and awareness. First find a comfortable spot to sit down and then put your healing stone(s) in your left hand and gently breathe in the fragrance of the essential oil(s). This ritual will help center you and reveal your inner child.

Next, call in the angels to open up your awareness to the world around you. Ask them to help you notice the small beauties and wonders of nature. With your jar or pouch in hand, go on a hunt for beautiful natural objects that catch your interest. You might be drawn to stones, shells, twigs, feathers, etc; just see what inspires you along the way. Don't worry about time; just be in the moment. After you collect your treasures, think of something creative and playful you can do with them at home.

Things to remember:

◆ Laugh

◆ Explore

◆ Be in the now

◆ Be silly

Forgiveness Field Trip

Reasons to take this trip: you are feeling resentful, angry, hurt, or heartbroken.

We have all been hurt by another's words and actions; sometimes we can let these hurts go, other times it is not so easy. If that person was especially important to us, we may harbor deep resentments. Over time these resentments eat away at us and turn into toxins in our energetic system. Our angels know that forgiveness is powerfully healing, so they encourage us to cleanse our system and renew our loving connections with those that have hurt us.

What you'll need:

◆ Pen and paper

◆ Healing stones (one or more)—opal, peridot, sugilite, rose quartz

◆ Essential oils (one or more)—sandalwood, Melissa, bergamot, rose, jasmine

◆ A selected spot in a wooded area or by the ocean; a large tree can also be used

When to start: morning, afternoon, or early evening, to be out in daylight

After you are in your nature spot, hold your healing stone(s) in your left hand and gently breathe in the fragrance of the essential oil(s). Call in the angels to assist you in the forgiveness process. Ask them to unblock the stuck energy in your heart chakra from holding on to hurt and resentment. You may feel a warm release in your heart area and then throughout your body.

Next, take your pen and paper and answer the following questions for each person you would like to forgive. If you are having trouble answering the questions, request that your angels help you get more in touch with your feelings and memories. After you have completed your questions, reread them and then say the following out loud or in your mind "I now transform the anger toward _____, which I have carried with me into a powerful energy of forgiveness. Forgiveness is now in my heart."

Things to remember:

 ◆ Forgiveness is powerfully healing

 ◆ Forgiveness opens your heart chakra

 ◆ Forgive yourself as you forgive others

Questions to ask yourself:

 ◆ What do I really feel hurt by?

 ◆ Before the person hurt me, they had many good qualities in my eyes. What are the good qualities that I remember?

 ◆ How has my resentment for this person negatively affected my life?

 ◆ How would forgiving this person positively affect my life?

Prosperity Field Trip

Reasons to take this trip: you are struggling, feeling helpless, or are experiencing a lack of abundance.

There are months, weeks, or even years where many of us are just getting by. We might be living from paycheck to paycheck and staying up at night worrying about money. It is times such as these that we are deep in the money woes. Hard financial times cannot be chalked up to bad luck or bad karma, for the Universe wants us to succeed. Cecily's teacher, Sonia Choquette, has said that we are all born as "trust fund babies of the Universe." It is just a matter of tapping into the pool of prosperity that is available to us all. We are all entitled to comfort and abundance, but many of us on some level do not feel we deserve it. Of course having money does not make you spiritually superior, it just means you feel you are worthy of a prosperous life. Your angel guides can show you how to feel rich, so you can bring more riches into your life.

What you'll need:

♦ Pen and paper

♦ Your nicest outfit and accessories

♦ Healing stones (one or more)—pyrite, tiger's eye

♦ Essential oils (one or more)—ginger, patchouli, cinnamon bark, bergamot

♦ Board game money

♦ A few affluent neighborhoods picked out

Leave behind: worries about bills and money

When to start: morning or afternoon (allow at least four hours) to be at your most awake and observant

Before you leave your home, hold your healing stone(s) in your left hand and gently breathe in the fragrance of the essential oil(s) to give you the energy of prosperity. Put your play money in your pocket to represent riches. Call in the angels to be by your side for encouragement as you spend your day as a wealthy person.

Now it is time to venture forth to your first affluent neighborhood. Spend the time as you would like going to upscale stores, cafés, car dealerships, hotels, and travel agencies. Walk through neighborhoods with large expensive houses and pick out your dream house. Remember: you will only be spending a minimum of money, as you are not making any large or extravagant purchases. This excursion is simply to help you feel prosperous and observe the prosperous energy in others.

Next, visit as many affluent neighborhoods as you wish. After your day out, you should feel invigorated and more confident. If you find that you are actually jealous or feeling sorry for yourself, ask the angels to give you more energy and positive expectations. When you arrive home, start a prosperity journal with the following questions. Going forward use this journal as a place to record all your dreams and express your feelings. You will find that the more you concentrate on positive expectations around your dreams, the quicker you will see abundance.

Things to remember:

◆ To prosper you must believe you are already prosperous

◆ Fake it until you make it

◆ The Universe wants us to be prosperous

Questions to ask yourself:

◆ How am I sabotaging my own prosperity?

◆ What positive qualities do I notice in those that are prosperous?

◆ What do I want in life? List material and nonmaterial desires. Be specific.

Parent and Child Field Trip

Reasons to take this trip: you want to have a playdate with the angels.

Children will love to find ways to connect with the angelic realm. There are some good reasons for this: First they can often see, hear, or feel the angels more frequently than adults. Secondly, the angels give them comfort and reassurance. Finally, they find the energy of the angels playful and fun to be around. The angels always welcome the time they can spend with us and our children, so be sure to set up a playdate.

What you'll need:

◆ Pen and paper

◆ Comfortable clothing

◆ Select a park or large field

◆ A blanket

◆ Picnic lunch or snacks

When to start: morning or afternoon, to be out in daylight

Go to the park or a large field and find a clean and comfortable spot with a good view of the sky. Spread your blanket out on the grass and lay on your backs. Call in the angels and ask for them to show themselves to you in the clouds. You will be hunting for the angels in the cloud formations. See how many angels you can find.

Next, use your imagination, intuition, and creativity to create a story together about your guardian angels. Write the story down and you can read it again and again as a bedtime story.

Things to remember:

◆ Children and the angels have a special kinship.

◆ The angels are playful.

◆ The wonders of the angels can be found everywhere.

Finding Your Spirit Field Trip

Reasons to take this trip: you are feeling uninspired, confused, empty, or stuck in a rut.

If we are to be fully alive, it is essential for us to find our spirit and nurture it. Our spirit is the core part of ourselves that is closest to God—it is untouched and pure. We cannot make contact with our spirit through our mind so we must depend on our heart and senses to lead us to our inner wisdom. The angels encourage us to get out of our head and into creative self-expression for our deepest spirit connection. They know that when we are in the flow of expressing ourselves we can only be in the moment, and this is exactly the place that we find our spirit.

What you'll need:

◆ Watercolors, finger paints, or crayons

◆ Water and a small paint brush for painting

◆ Paper

◆ Pen and journal

- Healing stones (one or more)—blue topaz, clear quartz, lapis, selenite

- Essential oils (one or more)—cedarwood, spruce, frankincense, sandalwood

- A beautiful spot in nature

When to start: morning or afternoon, to be out in daylight

Go to your beautiful nature spot, hold your healing stone(s) in your left hand, and gently breathe in the fragrance of the essential oil(s). Call in the angels to enhance your inspiration and intuition. Ask them to help you be in the moment fully engaged in self-expression. Pick up your paint brush, crayon, or use your paint-filled fingers and start drawing anything you like. Use the colors that speak to you. Do not be afraid of making a mistake. You are simply expressing what is in your spirit, so there is never any pressure to create an artistic masterpiece. You may become inspired or notice a particular peacefulness that washes over you as you are fully engaged in creating. Paint or draw as many pictures as you want. Next, move on to your spirit journal and answer the following questions. You may also feel like writing a story, poem, or song about your spirit. Keep the journal as a sacred place for self-expression and connection with your inner wisdom.

Things to remember:

- You need to feed your spirit every day.

- Self-expression is the key to finding your spirit.

- Your spirit is the real you; it is your authentic and wise self.

Questions to ask yourself:

- What inspires me?

- What does my spirit say?

- What activities make me feel fully alive?

- How can I be more creative in my daily life?

Romantic Love Field Trip

Reasons to take this trip: you are feeling lonely, frustrated in finding love, or ready to find the "one."

Romantic love is often a key to our growth and expansion as a person. A good and healthy relationship supports and encourages our soul growth and expands our capacity to love others. As human beings, we crave intimacy and want someone to open our hearts to. For those of us on a spiritual path, we desire more than just a companion, we want a true soulmate and spiritual partner. It is possible to achieve that powerful soul connection with another, when we are willing to surpass the person that we are today. Through growth on every level of our being, we are able to open a sacred space for an extraordinary love to come into our lives. The angels strive to be heavenly matchmakers by creating synchronicities and guiding us to open ourselves to the opportunities of love around us.

What you'll need:

- ◆ A journal and a pen
- ◆ Healing stones (one or more)—rose quartz, ruby
- ◆ Essential oils (one or more)—ylang ylang, rose, jasmine
- ◆ A destination popular with couples

Leave behind: the belief that you are unlucky in love

When to start: morning, afternoon, or evening

Before you leave your home, hold your healing stone(s) in your left hand and gently breathe in the fragrance of the essential oil(s). This ritual will enhance your ability to be open to love and recognize what you want in a soulmate. Call in your angels to accompany you on your outing. Ask them to help you sharpen your love radar, intuition, and awareness.

Go to a popular "couple's spot," make yourself comfortable, and then subtly observe those around you. Do not worry about being solo amongst a sea of couples. Trust and know that you will be in a wonderful soulmate relationship soon. Watch and listen to find examples of the type of love and relationships you desire and would like to emulate. Take your love journal and write down each quality that you are looking for in a soulmate as they pop into your head. You will intuitively know when you have captured the right information in your journal.

When you arrive home from your excursion, answer the following questions and then read Chapter 12 and use your love journal to complete the angels' method for calling in the "one."

Things to remember:

♦ Each of us deserves a loving and nurturing romantic relationship.

♦ The angels can help us enhance our love radar.

♦ Personal growth is an important key to remarkable love.

Questions to ask yourself:

♦ What do I have to share with a soulmate?

♦ What do I want to share with a soulmate?

♦ What would a day be like with my true soulmate?

♦ In what areas do I need to grow so I can be the best partner I can to another?

Gratitude Field Trip

Reasons to take this trip: you are ready to acknowledge and give thanks for all the good in your life.

Happiness is elusive without gratitude. Author Melody Beattie says, "Gratitude unlocks the fullness in life." You could say that gratitude is the key to a happy life that we hold in our hands, because if we are not grateful, none of the abundance we receive in our life will ever be enough for us. If we take our blessings for granted, we will always be looking for more things to fill our perceived emptiness. It is important that we keep our eyes peeled for the hidden riches in life, as well. The angels know that we must embrace and be grateful for our successes, as well as our failures, as each is a gift from the Divine. For what may not seem like a gift today, may come to be our greatest treasure.

What you'll need:

- A journal and pen
- Essential oils (one or more)—myrrh, frankincense, ylang ylang
- Friends or family to accompany you
- Your favorite place

When to start: morning, afternoon, or evening

When you meet up with your loved ones, ask each of them to gently breathe in the fragrance of the essential oil(s). Call in the angels to fill each of your hearts with the green and pink light of gratitude. Go to your absolute favorite place and form a circle or sit across from one another. In your own journals or with pen and paper, answer the following questions. After you each have a list of things that you are grateful for, take turns sharing them with each other. When you have each expressed gratitude, join hands and say "thank you" together.

Things to remember:

- When we live with love, grace, and gratitude, we find happiness.
- Gratitude helps us accept our past, find peace in the moment, and set dreams for the future.
- Bring an attitude of gratitude into your daily life.

Things to ask yourself:

- How have I taken certain blessings for granted?
- Name all the blessings in your life.
- Name all the blessings you have had today.

Finding Courage Field Trip

Reasons to take this trip: you are feeling scared, unsure, or struggling with a lack of self-confidence.

Sometimes it takes all we have to muster up courage for life's challenges. We may feel ill prepared or frightened when life's curve balls are thrown our way. Yet, to grow we must take risks and step outside our comfort zone. The angels want to help and know that finding courage can be one of the most empowering and beautiful things we can do in our lives.

What you'll need:

♦ Pen and paper

♦ Healing stones (one or more)—carnelian, hematite

♦ Essential oils (one or more)—clove, fennel, ginger, valor by Young Living (a mix of essential oils that enhances courage)

♦ A place of power (one with lots of mana, or life force energy) near a body of water, trees, or mountains

When to start: morning or afternoon, to be out in daylight

Go to your power spot in nature, hold your healing stone(s) in your left hand, and gently breathe in the fragrance of the essential oil(s). Call in the angels to enhance your personal power. Ask them to help you find your innate courage that emanates from your solar plexus chakra. Breathe deeply 12 times. Next, answer the following questions with pen and paper. After the questions have been answered, visualize the angels sending you mana from the earth and nature surrounding you. You may see the mana as a bright white light or it may be colored energy—whatever you see is appropriate. When you are fully charged with mana, you will feel calm yet empowered. To finish this field trip, plan an activity or take a class in the next month that you have always wanted to do, but were too scared to do it.

Things to remember:

♦ When we take risks, we live a fuller life.

♦ We all have courage inside of us, we just need to tap into it.

Questions to ask yourself:

♦ What are my fears?

♦ In what areas do I feel ill prepared?

- When have I shown courage in the past?
- What would my life be like if I took more risks and found my courage?

New Beginnings Field Trip

Reasons to take this trip: you are feeling ready for a change, inspired, and filled with positive expectations.

As we go through life, there are many seasons, phases, and cycles that we experience. Change and growth are part of our journey here on Earth and often new beginnings just show up for us. Yet there are times when we feel stagnant and yearn for movement, momentum, and something new. Most of the time to welcome the new in, we must leave those things in our lives that no longer serve us behind. Our angel guides can assist us in moving forward and help us discover new joys and surprises in our daily lives.

What you'll need:

- New clothes and new shoes
- Journal and pen
- Blank sheets of paper for burning
- Scissors
- Burning bowl (nonflammable, usually ceramic or stone), a lighter, sand or water to extinguish fire
- Healing stones (one or more)—azurite, citrine, golden calcite
- Essential oils (one or more)—peppermint, lemon, frankincense
- A new and beautiful place in nature you have never been to (find one that allows you to light a fire); use your backyard as an alternative location

When to start: morning or afternoon, to be out in daylight

Go to your beautiful nature spot, hold your healing stone(s) in your left hand, and gently breathe in the fragrance of the essential oil(s).

Call in the angels to inspire you and help you shed old, unwanted energies. Breathe deeply 12 times. Next, write down all the things that you would like to get rid of in your life. Take the scissors and cut out a strip of paper for each thing you have chosen.

For your next step, put a small amount of water or sand at the bottom of your bowl. Look at the first strip of paper and use the lighter to set a corner of it on fire. When the strip is lit, drop it into the burning bowl to extinguish the flame. Repeat with each strip of paper. (If a flame comes up from the bowl, dowse with water or sand.) After the fire ritual is complete, write down in your journal all the things that you want to bring into your life and then visualize the angels sending you inspiration and positive energy for the new beginnings that are coming to you.

Things to remember:

+ A brand-new start is priceless.

+ We are never trapped; there are always opportunities for new beginnings.

Appendix E

Resources

Hopefully this book has answered most of your questions about the angels—what they are, how to communicate with them, and how they can make your life better. However, we understand that learning isn't a destination, but a journey. The following books and websites will help you learn more about communicating with your angels, as well as provide more detailed information about other topics we mention in this book.

Books

Badonsky, Jill. *The Nine Modern Day Muses (and a Bodyguard): 10 Guides to Creative Inspiration for Artists, Poets, Lovers, and Other Mortals Wanting to Live a Dazzling Existence.* New York: Gotham Books, 2001.

Biziou, Barbara. *The Joy of Ritual: Recipes to Celebrate Milestones, Transitions, and Everyday Events in Our Lives.* Golden Books Adult Publishing, 1999.

Cameron, Julia. *The Artist's Way: A Spiritual Path to Higher Creativity.* New York: Tarcher/Putnum, 1992.

Chapman, Wendy H., and Carolyn Flynn. *The Complete Idiot's Guide to Indigo Children.* Indianapolis: Alpha Books, 2007.

Chopra, Deepak. *Power Freedom and Grace: Living from the Source of Lasting Happiness.* San Rafael, California: Amber-Allen Publishing, 2006.

Choquette, Sonia. *Ask Your Guides.* Carlsbad, California: Hay House Publishers, 2007.

———. *Diary of a Psychic.* Carlsbad, California: Hay House Publishers, 2003.

———. *The Psychic Pathway.* New York: Three Rivers Press, 1995.

———. *True Balance.* New York: Three Rivers Press, 2000.

———. *Trust Your Vibes.* Carlsbad, California: Hay House Publishers, 2005.

———. *The Wise Child.* New York: Three Rivers Press, 1999.

Cooper, Diana. *A Little Light on Angels.* Scotland, United Kingdom: Findhorn Press, 1997.

Dyer, Wayne W. *There's A Spiritual Solution to Every Problem.* New York: Harper Collins Books, 2001.

Emoto, Masaru. *The Hidden Messages in Water.* New York: Atria, 2005.

Foundation For Inner Peace. *A Course In Miracles.* Mill Valley, California: Foundation For Inner Peace, 1992.

Gaynor, Mitchell. *Sounds of Healing: A Physician Reveals the Therapeutic Power of Sound, Voice, and Music.* New York: Broadway, 1999.

Griswold, Mark, Barbara Griswold, and Trudy Griswold. *Angelspeake.* New York: Simon & Schuster, 1995.

Hay, Louise L. *You Can Heal Your Life.* Carlsbad, California: Hay House Publishers, 1984.

Hicks, Esther, and Jerry Hicks. *Ask and It Is Given: Learning to Manifest Your Desires.* Carlsbad, California: Hay House Publishers, 2004.

———. *The Law of Attraction: The Basics of the Teachings of Abraham.* Carlsbad, California: Hay House Publishers, 2006.

Keyes, Laurel Elizabeth. *Toning: The Creative Power of the Voice.* New York: DeVorss & Company, 1973.

Laroche, Loretta. *Life Is Short—Wear Your Party Pants: Ten Simple Truths That Lead to an Amazing Life.* Carlsbad, California: Hay House Publishers, 2003.

Linn, Denise. *Altars: Bringing Sacred Shrines Into Your Everyday Life.* New York: Ballantine Wellspring, 1999.

Michelle, Tina. *Sometimes It's the Journey ... Not the Destination.* Kearney, Nebraska: Morris Publishing, 2000.

Morgan, Marlo. *Mutant Message Down Under.* New York: Harper Collins Publishers, 1991.

Ray, Sondra. *Pele's Wish: Secrets of the Hawaiian Masters and Eternal Life.* Maui, Hawaii: Inner Ocean Publishing, 2005.

Roberts, Jane. *The Nature of Personal Reality.* New York: Bantam Books, 1974.

———. *Seth Speaks.* New York: Bantam Books, 1972.

Roman, Sanaya. *Living with Joy: Keys to Personal Power and Spiritual Transformation.* Novato, California: HJ Kramer, 1986.

———. *Personal Power Through Awareness.* Novato, California: HJ Kramer, 1986.

———. *Soul Love: Awakening Your Heart Centers.* Novato, California: HJ Kramer, 1997.

Roman, Sanaya, and Duane Packer. *Creating Money: Keys to Abundance.* Novato, California: HJ Kramer, 1988.

———. *Opening to Channel: How to Connect with Your Guide.* Novato, California: HJ Kramer, 1987.

———. *Spiritual Growth.* Novato, California: HJ Kramer, 1989.

Tamura, Michael J. *You Are The Answer: Discovering and Fulfilling Your Soul's Purpose.* Woodbury, Minnesota: Llewellyn, 2007.

Taylor, Terry Lynn. *Messengers of Light.* Novato, California: HJ Kramer, 1993.

Twyman, James F. *Emissary of Love: The Psychic Children Speak to the World*. Charlottesville, Virginia: Hampton Roads Publishing, 2002.

————. *The Moses Code: The Most Powerful Manifestation Tool in the History of the World*. Carlsbad, California: Hay House Publishers, 2008.

Virtue, Doreen. *Angel Medicine*. Carlsbad, California: Hay House Publishers, 2005.

————. *Angel Therapy: Healing Messages for Every Area of Your Life*. Carlsbad, California: Hay House Publishers, 1997.

————. *Healing with the Angels*. Carlsbad, California: Hay House Publishers, 1999.

————. *The Lightworker's Way*. Carlsbad, California: Hay House Publishers, 1997.

————. *Messages from Your Angels*. Carlsbad, California: Hay House Publishers, 2003.

————. *The Miracles of Archangel Michael*. Carlsbad, California: Hay House Publishers, 2008.

Williamson, Marianne. *The Gift of Change: Spiritual Guidance for Living Your Best Life*. New York: Harper San Francisco, 2004.

Oracle Cards

Choquette, Sonia. *Ask Your Guides Oracle Cards*. Carlsbad, California: Hay House Publishers, 2005.

Cooper, Diana. *Angel Cards for Children*. Scotland, United Kingdom: Findhorn Press, 2004.

————. *Teen Angels: 52-Card Deck*. Scotland, United Kingdom: Findhorn Press, 2005.

Marooney, Kimberly. *Angel Blessings: Cards of Sacred Guidance and Inspiration*. Beverley, Massachusetts: Fair Winds Press, 2001.

————. *Angel Love: Cards of Divine Devotion, Faith, and Grace*. Beverley, Massachusetts: Fair Winds Press, 2004.

Tyler, Kathy. *Angel Cards.* Asheville, North Carolina: Innerlinks, 1983.

Virtue, Doreen. *Archangel Oracle Cards.* Carlsbad, California: Hay House Publishers, 2004.

———. *Healing with the Angels Oracle Cards.* Carlsbad, California: Hay House Publishers, 1999.

———. *Healing with the Fairies Oracle Cards.* Carlsbad, California: Hay House Publishers, 2001.

———. *Messages from Your Angels Cards.* Carlsbad, California: Hay House Publishers, 2002.

Websites

www.acupuncturetoday.com—Online version of the acupuncture news publication, *Acupuncture Today.*

www.angelspeake.com—Home of author and teacher Trudy Griswold, where you can learn about her books, listen to the radio show, and follow the tour schedule.

www.angeltherapy.com—Doreen Virtue's Angel Therapy Practitioner Certification and Medium Certification. The website of Doreen Virtue, angel expert and Cecily's long-time mentor.

www.ashanamusic.com—The home of spiritual artist Ashana. Visit here to sample her music, learn more about her, or find out about tour information.

www.bachcentre.com—The healing flower techniques of late UK doctor Edward Bach.

www.charlesvirtue.com—Charles Virtue's Angel Certification Program. The website of Charles Virtue, angel expert and son of Doreen Virtue.

www.childrenofthenewearth.com—Children of the New Earth, a website for and about intuitive children.

www.crystalbowls.com—Crystal bowls from the company Crystal Tones.

www.dianacooper.com—The Diana Cooper School On Angels. Author of 17 books, Diana Cooper is one of the preeminent authorities on the angels and spirituality.

www.divineartistry.com—Cecily Channer's spiritual website.

www.emofree.com—Techniques and research on emotional freedom.

www.harpmagic.com—The home of award-winning harpist Peter Sterling. Background, music samples, and tour info are available on the site.

www.healthjourneys.com—Guided imagery from Belleruth Naparstek, a licensed social worker and spiritual practitioner.

www.heartmath.com—A world-renowned research facility, Heartmath studies the effect of spirituality, emotion, and other factors on human health.

www.jamestwyman.com—Website of peace troubadour James Twyman, a musician and a leader at the World Community of Saint Francis.

www.joanwanderson.com—Home of angel expert and author Joan Wester Anderson.

www.kimberlymarooney.com—Reverend Kimberly Marooney, Ph.D., discusses angelic guidance, spiritual healing, and her books on the site.

www.masaru-emoto.net—Website of Japanese spiritual researcher Masaru Emoto.

www.michaeltamura.com—Michael Tamura's Clairvoyant Training Program. Owners of the company Seraphim at Mt. Shasta, Michael and Raphaelle Tamura publish books, conduct seminars, and provide consulting on the angels.

www.naha.org—The official website of the National Association for Holistic Aromatherapy (NAHA).

www.nqa.org—The National Qigong Association. Dedicated to the ancient balanced health regimen from China.

www.reiki.org—The International Center for Reiki Training website.

www.ronnastar.com—Online home of Ronna Star, channel for the Archangel Michael.

www.soniachoquette.com—Sonia Choquette's Six Sensory Certification. One of Cecily's mentors, Sonia Choquette is an internationally respected expert on the angels, spirit guides, and related understandings.

www.soundhealingnetwork.org—The Sound Healing Network, an international community of sound healers.

www.terrylynntaylor.com—An angel card specialist and author, Terry Lynn Taylor provides wisdom and insights through her website.

www.tinamichelle.com—Tina Michelle's Discovering Your Enlightenment Spiritual Learning Series. A longtime mentor to Cecily, spiritualist Tina Michelle wrote the foreword to this book.

www.youngliving.us—The home of Young Living Essential Oils.

Index

I-J-K